The Foreign Policies
of the French Left

Other Titles in This Series

Westview Special Studies in West European Politics and Society

The Foreign Policies of the French Left
edited by Simon Serfaty

A series of seminars held in the winter of 1977-78 at the Washington Center of Foreign Policy Research, Johns Hopkins School of Advanced International Studies, provided the basis for the material collected in this book. At the time of the seminars, a victory of the Left in the March 12 and 19 elections was being widely predicted, and the authors were encouraged to speculate on the probable foreign policy implications for France should that victory be realized. The Left did not sweep the elections as predicted, but these revised and updated essays remain valuable, first because of the constraints that a nearly even distribution of political forces imposes on the existing majority, and second because future Leftist participation in the French government will undoubtedly lead to a renewal of such speculations in the years ahead.

Simon Serfaty provides an overview of the domestic situation in France since Valery Giscard d'Estaing became president in 1974, and the following chapters successively deal with the Left's outlook on Europe, the Atlantic Alliance, and the Third World. The book ends with an examination of the impact the French Left has had and may continue to have on Eastern communism.

Simon Serfaty is associate professor of international relations and director of the Washington Center of Foreign Policy Research, Johns Hopkins School of Advanced International Studies.

The Foreign Policies
of the French Left
edited by Simon Serfaty

Westview Press / Boulder, Colorado

Westview Special Studies in
West European Politics and Society

Copyright © 1979 by Westview Press, Inc.

Published in 1979 in the United States of America by
     Westview Press, Inc.
     5500 Central Avenue
     Boulder, Colorado 80301
     Frederick A. Praeger, Publisher

Library of Congress Catalog Card Number: 79-53137
ISBN: 0-89158-652-0

Composition for this book was provided by the author.
Printed and bound in the United States of America.

Contents

Preface

The essays included in this volume were written
for a series of seminars which took place at the
Washington Center of Foreign Policy Research of the
Johns Hopkins School of Advanced International Studies. Held at a time when a victory of the Left was
widely expected in the legislative elections of
March 12 and 19, 1978, the series reflected the Center's continuing interest in the changing international environment of American foreign policy. As
it is well known, such predictions did not come to
pass. Yet, these essays, revised and updated, remain eminently useful for reasons which should become all too evident in the pages that follow.

The authors are very appreciative of the numerous constructive comments made by all those who par-
ticipated in our seminars. We are also indebted to
Sharon Bourne Newman who prepared the manuscript
with her usual typing skill and professional
diligence.

Simon Serfaty,
Director, The Washington Center
of Foreign Policy Research,
School of Advanced
International Studies

ix

About the Contributors

SIMON SERFATY is an Associate Professor of International Relations and Director of the Washington Center of Foreign Policy Research at Johns Hopkins School of Advanced International Studies. His most recent book After Thirty Years: A Fading Partnership? will appear later this year.

MICHAEL M. HARRISON is an Assistant Professor of European Studies at the Johns Hopkins School of Advanced International Studies. He has recently completed a book entitled The Reluctant Ally: France and the Atlantic Alliance, to be published shortly, and is currently collaborating with Dr. Serfaty on a study of the security perspectives of the left in France and Italy funded by the Ford Foundation.

J. WILLIAM FRIEND, now retired, was a senior analyst with the Central Intelligence Agency. He has written widely on the French Communist Party and is currently working on a book about Italian foreign policy.

RONALD TIERSKY is an Associate Professor of Political Science at Amherst College. The author of French Communism, 1920-1974, he is currently working on a study of democratic centralism and Eurocommunism which should be published in 1980.

PAVEL MACHALA is an Assistant Professor of Political Science at Amherst College. Having recently published an article, "Eastern Europe, Eurocommunism and the Problems of Detente" in Many Faces of Communism, ed. Morton Kaplan, he is completing a new book, Marx on International Political Economy.

1
The Fifth Republic
under Valery Giscard D'Estaing

Simon Serfaty

Political games in France abound once again.
On the side of the government, a declining Gaullist
party--still the majority of the majority--emerges
as President Giscard d'Estaing's most vociferous
critic, even while refusing adamantly to heed
Michel Debré's call to enter into the opposition.
On the side of the opposition, a declining Communist Party (PCF)--now the minority party of the mi-
nority--focuses its harshest criticism on its Socialist ally (PS), even while it continues to pro-
claim its faith in the Union de la Gauche. Already
without a program worth fighting for, the Union
finds no integrated program it can fight against
either, as the majority's "programme de Blois" of
January 1978 is equally forgotten. Accordingly,
the Socialists and the Communists actively consolidate their defeat of March 1978, adding bitter internal quarrels to the many conflicts that separate
them. Similarly, however, the Gaullists and the
Giscardistes reserve their sharpest barbs for each
other: as Jacques Chirac warns against the "foreign party" which, through its support for Europe,
promotes the economic subjugation and the international impotence of France, Giscard's spokesman be-
moans the irresponsibility of those whose excessive
ambitions and absurd tactics help revive anti-
German xenophobic tendencies and other old demons.[1]
As the seventies come to an end, a victorious Right
escapes its divisions through a rosy contemplation
of the future: the next century for Giscard, the
next presidential elections for Chirac, and the
next decade for Barre. As to the Left, it broods
over its present misfortunes possibly at the expense of a future that appears to be increasingly
compromised: "The Left will never win," proclaims
a widely read book in France.[2] In the meanwhile,

1

though, the barons of the PCF and of the PS limit their "great debates" to whether dissent within the former should express itself in the pages of L'Humanité or Le Matin, or whether former divisions within the latter represent "factions" or "tendencies." Poor Left, poor Right, poor France: where in 1977-1978 the struggle was over projects of society, it is, in 1979-1980, over semantics and timetable.

I

The erosion of the majority, as shaped by de Gaulle and preserved by Georges Pompidou, was expected under Giscard. If in the sixties Gaullism effectively found in the enlargement of the Cold War cage some room for a national role in the grandes affaires, it sought less successfully at home a framework within which a similar nonpartisan consciousness might actually permit a consensus over domestic policies as well.[3] Initially, of course, such a consensus could easily be generated by de Gaulle himself. The Good General and the General Good were for France one and the same, linked by the "great people brought together" against the discredited political parties, including the Gaullist party itself, one which de Gaulle tolerated rather than led. In those days, the Fifth Republic was neither a regime nor a constitution, but a man, as many observers noted. But with de Gaulle's withdrawal in early 1969, and his replacement by a dauphin chosen the previous summer when Pompidou's dismissal had promoted him as a credible substitute, the Fifth Republic became dependent on a political party--l'Etat UDR--which promptly built a partisan consciousness that found the opposition at its nadir at the 1969 presidential elections.

Throughout, however, the Gaullist efforts to remain a national movement and a partisan movement were self-contradictory. Already in the sixties, the Gaullists had emphasized both the perfection of the new institutions (namely, the Constitution of 1958 as amended in 1962) and the indispensability of their leader. But, as the opposition predictably argued, if the institutions were as solid as they were said to be, why could they not survive a change of leadership? The political debate, then, was over the regime itself--not an unusual occurrence in France where the opposition has generally not confined itself to the sole criticism of policy.

2

Over time, however, given the continued public support for the institutions of the Fifth Republic, a
support which grew further even following de
Gaulle's withdrawal, the Socialists and the Communists too concluded, between February 1968 and June
1972, that the existing constitution, however "un-
finished," was nevertheless the best available.
Hence the apparent end of the guerre des répub-
liques, as Jacques Chaban Delmas once called it, as
the political game could now take place within the
existing constitutional framework.[4] In the seventies therefore the political debate centered on the
very nature of the French society--a guerre des
projets, as it came to be.

     As an antipartisan consciousness, Gaullism
could, and did, easily survive de Gaulle's death.
As a partisan political force it could not, and did
not, survive Pompidou's death. From the beginning
a majority party before it became a party at all,
the UDR wanted to achieve a closer identification
with the general (to increase its electoral gains)
while maintaining a certain distance from him (to
facilitate its survival). Under de Gaulle the party received its impetus from the charismatic presence of its heroic leader. Under Pompidou, such
impetus was not lost but now stemmed from a widespread sense of prosperity as well as from the fear
of an alternative which the nation had tasted and
discarded in May 1968. Following Pompidou's death,
the party could find neither a compelling leadership nor a distinct identity out of its many so-
called "barons," including former Prime Ministers
Pierre Messner, Jacques Chaban Delmas, and Michel
Debré. Thus, the electorate would perceive neither
the difference between Giscard and Chaban, nor the
"adventurism" of the Common Program: it was now
possible to vote against the Gaullist candidate
without voting against Gaullism (or to vote for
Mitterrand without voting against the regime).
Similarly, once elected, Giscard could initially
ignore the Gaullist deputies (minimally represented
in his first government) without being opposed by
them. Yet, aware of the necessity to cultivate his
parliamentarian majority if he were to preserve his
presidential majority, Giscard urged Chirac to control and contain the UDR's divisions of early 1974,
a task which appeared to be fulfilled with Chirac's
forceful seizure of the party's presidency.

     But how long could Chirac and the Gaullists
remain satisfied by such a status quo? The answer
became rapidly obvious to both men who soon emerged

as enemy partners of sorts, mixing in a strange way
true kinship and growing personal and political
hostility. In 1974, without Chirac, Giscard would
not have been president; but without Giscard,
Chirac would not have risen so quickly as a potential substitute. In 1975, Chirac could not see
Giscard fail yet, for the Left might then prove
difficult to displace; but Chirac could not see
Giscard succeed either, for then Giscard might himself prove difficult to replace. By 1976, Giscard
could not easily govern without Chirac, but he
could not preside with him; similarly, Chirac could
govern under Giscard, but he could not preside with
him.

In the past to be sure, there had been disagreements between the president and his prime minister: de Gaulle had found it necessary to replace
Debré; and Pompidou, Chaban. Also the leader of
the majority party, the president could dismiss his
prime minister at will. Unlike his predecessors
at the Elysée, however, Giscard was not the legitimate head of the majority party of the majority--
his first prime minister was. Of course, Giscard
could still terminate him, as he ultimately did on
August 25, 1976; but as it was seen subsequently,
this might be done at the cost of his majority.

In March 1976, the cantonal elections came as
a shock to the president and "his" majority as the
Left made impressive gains (194 additional seats
for the Socialists alone) which widely confirmed
the perceived disarray of the majority. To the
Gaullists such dismal performance (a loss of 36
seats for the Giscardistes) was a further evidence
of Giscard's inability to lead the institutions
which he had borrowed from them. Their unrest
therefore increased all the more markedly as Chirac,
allegedly Giscard's viceroy, was no longer either
willing or able to preserve the unity of the majority behind the president. The political future of
the prime minister and that of the Gaullist party,
pledged by him to a prompt return to power, had to
be saved against the president as well as against
the rise of the parties of the opposition. In
earlier years, Gaullism had been built around de
Gaulle's idée de la France. Giscard and Mitterrand
now wanted to replace it with une idée des Français,
an "idea" which was deemed to be wrong, in Giscard's
case because it overstated France's passion for
moderation, and in Mitterrand's case because it
overstated France's need for change. Instead, the
leader of the UDR sought a relaunching of Gaullism

4

on the basis of une idée de Chirac: to be, in his own words, a "rampart against weakness," not only the weakness of Giscard against the Left, but also that of Mitterrand against the Communists. As of the spring of 1976, therefore, the Gaullists answered--however belatedly--Giscard's never forgotten "yes-but" to de Gaulle with a "no-but" of their own.

Not surprisingly, in contrast to the divisions of the majority, the rise of the Left, apparently united over program and leadership, and oblivious of past quarrels over its ideological legacy, seemed to be irresistible, as confirmed by the steadfastness of the polls throughout 1977 and early 1978, even following the September split between the PS and the PCF.

II

Yet, neither the Communists nor the Socialists ever reconciled themselves to the strategy of union. It was said to be a "permanent struggle," as Georges Marchais put it in Le Monde on October 13, 1977: but a struggle against whom if not Mitterrand, and against what if not the union itself? Going beyond its early, personalized attacks against Mitterrand ("increasingly self-assured and domineering," as stated by the party's secretary in early February 1975), the PCF proved soon to be embittered over the electoral gains of the PS. "Victory for the Left," Marchais predicted in mid-1975,"could not be built on the basis of a weakening of the Communist Party and of the influence of its ideas on the working class." Seemingly, the Communists were already assuming then that they were owed the full allegiance of the working masses still influenced by the bourgeois corruptability of the PS, likely to remain, as the PCF saw it, "what it is, namely, a traitor."[5] It was further hoped that the public impact of an escalated rhetoric of showdown with the PS could be neutralized by the soothing effect of a Eurocommunist rhetoric of reconciliation: hence the then surprising accord in Rome with Berlinguer in October 1975, and the subsequent attacks, unprecedented at the time, against Moscow over the question of labor camps--"all the fuss," as a member of the Soviet Politburo put it in Nanterre in February 1976, "about the rights of man in socialist society."[6]

Yet, while unable to live together peacefully,

5

the PCF and the PS could not live separately
either. For, however difficult it may be for the
Left to win when united, it is even less likely to
succeed when disunited. The PS needed the PCF to
do away with the Mollet legacy and legitimate its
socialism; the PCF needed the PS to do away with
the Thorez legacy and legitimate its national identity. Without the PCF, the PS could find a majority only through a turn to the center: it could
then govern, but only at the cost of its stated,
ideological raison d'être. Otherwise, it was but
one of two minorities on the left. Similarly,
without the PS, the PCF could only move to its
left, thereby confirming its revolutionary tradition, but at the cost of its national legitimacy.
In other words, without the PCF, the PS could not,
and cannot, be both a socialist party and a party
of the majority; without the PS, the PCF was, and
is, neither a liberated party nor a party of the
majority. Ironically, the same considerations of
power that made the alliance possible in 1972, also
made the rupture possible in 1977. For while
Georges Marchais reasoned that Mitterrand was weak-
ened by his commitment to the acquisition of power
over anything else (and thus was sensitive to Communist pressures), François Mitterrand too felt
all the more capable of resisting such pressures as
he perceived--"I don't calculate, I feel," he has
written in his journal[7]--a similar commitment on
the part of his adversary ally. Needless to say,
both Mitterrand and Marchais proved to be wrong.
    The Common Program was an electoral platform
that preceded the crisis of the seventies. While
no one was forgotten and everything was promised,
no attempt was made to make it operational. Re-
reading it, one is struck by the superficiality of
the analysis and the lack of any specific policy.
It was a projet de programme for a projet de société, one which remained for several years the most
debated and the least known political document in
France. Up to 1976, only one book (Soisson's Le
Piège) could be said to review systematically the
substance and implications of the program. Even
during the 1975 presidential contest references to
the Common Program were made more often by Giscard
than by Mitterrand who referred to it briefly no
more than three times in the course of ten tele-
vision appearances throughout the campaign.[8]
    Only the intensification of the PCF's attacks
against the PS following the break of September 23
forced the public to focus on the Program itself.

6

This, however, spelled electoral disaster since the Program itself was neither credible nor desirable to the more marginal voters of the Center who feared the risks written into it more than the changes which it promised. "Everything is not always possible all the time," had reflected Mitterrand on April 15, 1975:[9] but (through such a banality) was he thinking of the Left in the thirties, as he writes he was, or was he already fearing for the Left in the seventies, as it is tempting to assume?

In any case, to speak of "a" program that was "common" to both major leftist parties was a gross oversimplification. There were at least two, and possibly three, Socialist interpretations of the 1972 agreement, and none of these matched the PCF's official or private understanding of it. Thus, while most at the PCF looked upon the Programme Commun as a minimal point of departure, most at the PS looked upon it as a maximal point of arrival. Privately, the PCF emphasized and compared Socialist reluctance and Communist expectations, even though publicly they ignored interparty differences and minimized their ambitions. Publicly the PS reaffirmed its ideological commitment, but privately it underlined its pragmatism. The PS wanted to let circumstances shape the application of the program and the evolution of the structures of the nation. The PCF expected to see circumstances shaped by the immediate transformation of these structures through the application of the Program. Thus, while Mitterrand downplayed the scope of the projected nationalizations, and dismissed the workers' proclaimed right to demand such nationalizations; while he emphasized his intention to compensate generously small and large shareholders alike; and while he conveniently placed the responsibility for the lingering influence of the Communist Party on the ineptitude and misguided policies of the existing majority, Michel Rocard confirmed the PS commitment to a market economy which would be strengthened by the Common Program, and Jean Pierre Chevènement argued essentially the reverse.[10] In the end, of course, the PCF's willingness to overlook its initial misgivings about Mitterrand, and pretend to go along with a more moderate analysis of the program failed to survive Marchais' determination to make "the PCF much stronger, much more influential," as he wrote in Le Monde of September 30, 1977.

Is it surprising then that the Left too proved to be doomed to failure?

Such failure was to be especially difficult to
face for the leadership as well as for the rank and
file. To be sure, there had been such losses before, and the electoral performance of the French
Left since the end of World War II speaks for itself: four governments with a Socialist prime minister under the Fourth Republic for a total dura-
tion of thirty-two months and eighteen days, followed by repeated setbacks during the Fifth Republic, including six legislative and three presidential elections. 1978, however, was widely expected
to bring a reversal of such misfortunes: circumstances could hardly have been any better. At home,
the publicly divided majority appeared to be an easy
prey, faced with high unemployment, low growth,
persistent inflation--and little relief in sight.
"Had there not been that economic crisis ...,"
lamented Giscard wistfully in March 1976, when con-
templating his performance since inauguration
day.[11] This, the "priority of priorities," was not
all: in 1976, the disintegration of the university,
the malaise in the army, the threatened bankruptcy
of the social security system, the conflict between
police and justice, the separatist agitation in
Corsica and in Brittany, made Giscard's successive
pleas for "decrispation" and "dedramatization" look
hopeless.[12] The Left was now moving into the driv-
er's seat all the more safely as abroad, detente
between the United States and the Soviet Union as
well as the elusive pull of Eurocommunism allowed
the Communist half of the Left to reclaim a national legitimacy which it had lost since 1947. All in
all, with polls consistently showing a steady six-
point margin in favor of the Union, most observers
had come to see Mitterrand's victory as nearly
inevitable.

That such forecast proved in the end to be
premature is well known. Prospects of success did
not only enhance further conflicts between the
Socialists and the Communists increasingly anxious
to prevent each other from gaining an ascendancy
which each party sought for itself. They also revived last minute misgivings within an electorate
which tends to shy away from the uncertainties written into the emergence of a governing coalition
that is still seen as unreliable and unpredictable.

Three considerations therefore help explain
the elections of March 1978. First, there was the
fear engendered by the perspective of a return of

the Communists to government. To a significant
number of Frenchmen a strong and domineering Communist Party was not a credible party yet. It remained historically compromised by thirty years of
systematic opposition to successive governments and
regimes, subservient allegiance to Moscow, and deplorable Stalinist internal structures. The reluctant adjustments of the previous five years were
not sufficient to alleviate a suspicion which
Georges Marchais' renewed aggressiveness in late
1977 had revived further. From this viewpoint,
there was no comparison possible between the French
party and its Italian counterpart in whose case the
party's electoral success was based on its national
and interclassist appeal as an efficient party of
law and order.

Combined with these apprehensions about the
Communists' role in a government of the left was a
growing fear of the PS programs. As it has been
said many times, France is a conservative country
with an occasionally revolutionary rhetoric. For
better or worse, the new society the French want
never is the "new society" which is offered to them
at any given time. For it then becomes a frighten-
ing form of adventurism.[13] Such concerns peaked in
early 1978 when the uncertainties which had surrounded the economic objectives of the PS were apparently clarified with the detailed publication
of its economic plan. To many the Socialist intentions were all the more "adventurist" (including,
for instance, an immediate 35 percent increase of
minimum wages much criticized, then and subsequently, by Rocard) as they were to be carried out on
the basis of an explicitly unstable political alliance, and in the midst of a generally hostile international setting.

Finally, there was a fear that the "Republican
order" might be threatened by a confrontation between a prime minister and a president who would
rely on two different and conflicting majorities
Such a concern was surprisingly enhanced by Giscard's closing speech of March 11, 1978. Prime
Minister Raymond Barre (who throughout the campaign
reminded the electorate of the enormous constitutional power of the president) and Chirac (who reduced the presidential alternatives in the aftermath of an eventual victory of the Left to two,
confrontation or resignation) had paved the way for
a presidential blackmail that threatened the voters
with the consequences of their own free choice, including the pointed promise of economic chaos.

Such pre-election calls had been made before--by de Gaulle and Pompidou alike--without any substantial impact on the projected outcome of the elections. But when combined with the doubts already raised by the Left--both as a whole and as a sum of its parts--Giscard's intervention emerged as a catalyst that was especially effective in the light of Giscard's own growing popularity: by early February 1978, the last pre-election poll testing his performance showed 56 percent of the sample as "satisfied" with Giscard, compared to 38 percent "dissatisfied."[14] Significantly enough, this was his best showing in two years.

Thus, once again, France voted in March 1978 less for the Right than against the Left; and she voted less against the Left than against this Left, a Left within which the Communists were deemed to be too influential. Paradoxically, the true election winner lost: this, after all, was the best performance of the Socialist Party in a legislative election since October 1945; it was also the first time since the end of World War II that it did better than the Communist Party; and it was the only party in France whose share of the popular vote in March 1978 increased when compared with the previous legislative elections. None of the other three major groupings could claim such progress, least of all the PCF whose performance was the second worst since 1945. "When I signed the Common Program in 1972," Mitterrand said in mid-March, "the Socialist Party had 11 percent of the vote. In 1973, at the time of the legislative elections it amounted to 19%. It amounts today to more than 23%." A meagre consolation indeed. For, as the Socialist leader himself put it on April 3, 1978-- "Since it was said that we were to win, it is therefore we who lost."[15]

IV

Not too much should be made out of the initial turmoil that unfolded within the PCF following the 1978 elections. Similar crises had arisen before-- after the Soviet invasion of Hungary, for instance, when many an intellectual left the party--without affecting significantly the PCF's positions and strategy. In other words, grand expectations about the party's propensity for change are likely to remain illusory: the evolution of the PCF is still limited by a legacy that statements about the

10

legitimacy of dissent in the Soviet Union and the
benefits of international detente cannot eliminate
easily. Yet, throughout the seventies, the French
Communists have displayed an unusual willingness to
at least permit a reconsideration of its past.
Jean Elleinstein, for example, finds in the weight
of history a heavy burden for the Communist Party
to carry. "Still today," he wrote in Le Monde on
April 3, 1978,

> the analysis of the realities of the Soviet
> Union remains very much below what is neces-
> sary ... The foreign policy of the Soviet
> Union is only rarely questioned ... [The So-
> viet Union] is neither a model nor an example,
> but ... an anti-model ... [The very name of
> the party] represents a heavy handicap vis a
> vis French opinion.

Jean Elleinstein today discovers the "failures" of
Soviet socialism with the same passion as he had
shown when discovering its "merits" thirty years
earlier. His guilty plea, whatever its passionate
form and whatever its empirical substance, is less
significant as the fact that such mea culpa does
not come together with an instant expulsion from
the party, as this would have been the case in the
past.
    In fact, in 1978 the party itself appeared at
first to endorse, in part at least, such analysis.
"More than other communist parties," it was thus
argued in a semi-official party book, the PCF was
sensitive to Soviet influence. It was wrong, write
the authors of L'URSS et Nous, to neglect "Stalin's
politico-ideological crimes and deviations"; to reject such "great personalities" as Trotski or Buk-
harin; or to delay the party's response to the XXth
Congress of the CPSU.[16] But, it is added, the
forces of reaction pressured the PCF into such attitudes, at home and abroad. How convenient! Before the war, we are told, the Popular Front,
Spain, Fascism, and Munich diverted the party's attention away from Stalin's excesses; after the war,
Stalin was a much needed symbol ("Il ne faut pas
désesperer Billancourt"); in 1956, there were the
colonial war in Algeria, the imperialist venture in
Suez, and the organized waves of anticommunism
everywhere. As to the one-party system in the
Soviet Union, it was the consequence of circumstances: the party was the only force able not only
to give society a new direction, but also, and more

11

fundamentally, to keep it alive. The subsequent
Stalinist excesses reflect the frailty of human behavior (party membership as the avenue to power)
rather than a failure of ideology. In sum, circumstances being different in France--and the party's
leadership less weak and less opportunistic--plu-
ralism would not be endangered.

The PC pleads guilty then, but with extenuat-
ing circumstances, and always with an opportunistic
eye on the implications which such historical precedents may have on the current political debate
in France. Thus, while the Communists organize
seminars on Algeria and cite the responsibility of
the PS in waging a war meant to preserve a French
Algeria, the Socialists organize seminars on Stalin
and quote the very authors of L'URSS et Nous (Fran-
cis Cohen, for example, who used to refer to Stalin
as "the highest scientific authority in the world").

To be sure the party's adjustments these past
few years have been numerous--from the disappearance of the dictatorship of the proletariat as a
party objective to the Declaration of Freedoms, and
from the numerous condemnations (although usually
conditional) of the Soviet regime to a belated endorsement of parliamentary institutions. The party is indeed being normalized--it is losing its
foreign identity and seeking a more liberal structure. But such normalization, however real it may
prove to be in the end, is proceeding grudgingly
and cannot yet wash away the rhetoric and the policies of the past. What was unanimously approved
one year earlier is unanimously rejected a year
later. Few and distant, changes remain "globally
negative," to parallel Marchais' overall assessment of the Soviet experience as being "globally
positive."[17] At the XXIIIrd Congress of May 1979,
the PC still presents only one resolution to be
voted on by the party representatives, and only one
proposal for the reforms of the statutes to be discussed in plenary session. Both, of course, are
offered by the party's secretary who, ironically
enough, refers to his proposals as "an open dé-
marche." Consequently, the more the PC speaks of
its commitment to changed internal structures and
policies, the more it enhances suspicions and dis-
satisfaction about its motivations and directions
as its continued decline in by-elections in late
1978 clearly shows.

More consequential is the post-March 1978
fragmentation of the PS. A modern Sisyphus, the
Socialist Party has waged uphill battles time and

again, and it has fallen time and again. But, unlike Camus' Sisyphus, it can no longer be thought
of happy in the aftermath of what Michel Rocard
called "the murder of an immense hope." At Epinay
in 1971, and at Pau in 1975, many came to Mitterrand as the only possible rallying point of a party
then in disarray. Their initial conversion (from
Chevènement's CERES at Epinay to Rocard's old PSU
at Pau) appeared to be justified by the electoral
progress of the PS, a progress that was all the
more exaggerated as the point of reference (Gaston
Defferre's presidential candidacy in 1969) proved to
be especially helpful. Other base years and other
criteria could have been used to show less dramatic
achievements: by 1974, for instance, the party's
membership was essentially the same as it was in
1957 (140,000), and while it grew somewhat during
the "golden years" (1974-1977) it still remained
slightly over half the party's membership in 1947
(160,000 now, as compared to 300,000 then).

Prior to the March 1978 elections, the various
divisions within the PS--divisions of ideology as
well as divisions of convenience--had remained,
with the exception of CERES, muted if not altogether underground. Since then, however, they have
surfaced with a vengeance. Indeed, Mitterrand
could easily make his own de Gaulle's reflection
of May 15, 1962: "What is to be feared [after my
withdrawal] ... is not a political void but rather
an overflow."

On the left of the party, CERES, embittered
over its expulsion from the PS majority in 1975, is
a party within the party, with a press of its own,
funds of its own, a structure and a leadership of
its own. From the September 23 break on, its criticism of Mitterrand's leadership and of those who,
as Chevènement put it in early November 1977, "ac-
commodate themselves too well of the rupture," became sharper and even more public than before.
Since the elections CERES, while showing some surprising divisions over the best strategy to adopt
toward Rocard and the PCF, has continued to seek
policies meant not only to facilitate the liberali-
zation of the Communist Party (through a firm commitment to the continuation of the union) but also
to prevent the social-democratization of the PS
(through its persistent critique of Mitterrand's
programatic ambiguities).

For the rest, however, the Socialist divisions
often seem to center more on personalities than on
substance as they grow out of a steady erosion of

13

Mitterrand's credibility within the party he helped
rebuild as well as within the nation he hoped to
lead. To many, this is long overdue: from himself
to himself the distance which Mitterrand has trav-
eled over the years is inhabited by too many ghosts
(even if he himself often but not always fought
them) and interrupted by too many defeats.[18] He,
who has refused to remain enslaved to a past ("The
only possible negotiation is war," he said of Algeria in 1956) or to a future (including the Common Program) is now caught into a present that he
cannot so easily evade. To keep control of the
party, Mitterrand may have to force its two most
popular figures (Rocard and Mauroy) into the minority, and possibly return to an alliance of sort
with CERES at the price of a new glissement à
gauche which would further compromise whatever
presidential aspirations he may still have. Mitterrand looks to Epinay to justify a plea for
"stricter rules of discipline" with a strong leadership. Rocard, who was not at Epinay, criticizes
the "nearly discretionary" authority of the party's
secretary and recommends instead a collegial lead-
ership--"at all levels"--for a mass party which
would regain its membership of the late forties.
    On such substantive issues as the rupture of
France with its capitalist structures, the differences are rhetorically sharper even though they remain pragmatically vague. Closer to Chevènement
than to Rocard, Mitterrand proclaims the need for
an instant rupture ("not to modernize capitalism,
or to moderate it, but to replace it with socialism") and the primacy of the plan over the market
("it will not be the market which insures the global regulation of the economy"). Speaking instead
of a "succession of ruptures" to be implemented in
the light of existing constraints, Rocard recog-
nizes the continued dominance of a market economy:
"the plan," he claims "promises to break with the
logic of profit, which is different from the logic
of market." And Mauroy to add: "The plan cannot ... completely dominate the market." All in
all, both Rocard and Mauroy agree, in Rocard's
words, that "the left cannot promise more than it
can deliver," while Mitterrand argues that not to
promise more is to promote the image of a party
which cannot do anything at all. Significantly,
no one questions the principle of an alliance with
the PCF, but no one specifically explains how such
an alliance can be made operative, unless much can
be made out of Mitterrand's call for "a pact of

14

nonaggression" between the two parties, as compared
to Rocard's "Finie l'union defensive." What such
differences on these and other domestic issues en-
tail in practice remains, of course, to be seen.[19]
    With a PCF that remains substantially short of
both, what it used to be and what it wants to be,
and with a PS that remains disunited around a man
more than around a program or an ideology, is it
excessive, then, to conclude that the future of the
French Left is as compromised under Giscard as it was
before him--unless, of course, the Right (Chirac)
does for the Left (Mitterrand or Rocard) in 1981
what the Left (Marchais) did for the Right (Giscard)
in 1978, thereby illustrating the true paradox of
the French Left, namely, that its electoral victory
is all the more likely as it remains unexpected?

                          V

    At first, the repoliticization of the Fifth
Republic under Giscard, which should by now be apparent, took place at the expense of the former
primacy of foreign policy. Possibly preoccupied
by the growing political challenge from the Left,
Giscard failed to show the same penchant for les
grandes affaires as de Gaulle and, to a lesser extent, Pompidou (although de Gaulle too had found it
necessary to postpone many of his major foreign
policy initiatives until settlement of various domestic issues, including the drafting of a constitution and the end of the Algerian war). Instead,
foreign policy was accepted reluctantly by Giscard
as one of the instruments which might help with the
"transformation and guidance of the [French] society" (December 22-23, 1974).* To be sure, Giscard
occasionally spoke of changing, however marginally,
the "design of the world."[20] Yet, the overall Gaullist ambition to transform single-handedly the international milieu generally vanished after 1974.
Au fond, the reshuffling which the general wished
to promote, and which Pompidou accepted to endure,
had not come out quite as expected. In the aftermath of the Yom Kippur War, the threat to the preservation and expansion of French interests came
from new and unforeseen sources previously said to

---

*For the balance of this section such dates refer
to the issue of Le Monde in which Giscard's statements are reported.

15

belong to the level of "low politics"--the price
and supply of oil, the scarcity of raw materials in
an otherwise overpopulated world, the disorganiza-
tion of world trade. According to Giscard, these
were "problems of human kind" (December 22-23,
1974). They forced the dependence of all on all
and required, if they were to be solved, a prise de
conscience supplémentaire entre les nations (October 26, 1974). Needless to say, Giscard's plane-
tary consciousness has been sharply influenced by
his political fortunes at home. When he found
France difficult to govern ("to manage the unpredictable," he complained in October 1974) he similarly found the world "unhappy" and without direction ("and should it know" where it is going, Giscard added, "it would be to discover that it is
going toward catastrophe.") While there were moments of euphoria in 1975-1977, there not to
be, significantly enough, any such moment of gloom
as of 1978.

Given this early focus on nonmilitary issues,
Giscard initially ignored questions of physical
security as rather incredible ("tres peu vrais-
semblable," October 26, 1974). Even the force de
frappe was said to be nothing more than "a phase"
(July 27, 1974) which was endured because "all
hypotheses must be covered." From 1975 on, however, the French president took on more Gaullist
tones. "We live," he declared on March 25, 1975,
"in a world which is still violent and in which
the problem of security is therefore raised." In
a "modern world which is a harsh world" (June 18,
1976) "all states must be able to protect themselves against ... eventualities which are an intrinsic part of international life" (February 9,
1978). Such eventualities are all the more real
as, unlike de Gaulle who saw the sources of international disorder move away from Europe, Giscard
saw them "coming closer to Europe" (March 27,
1975). France, Giscard now argued, "must have an
independent defense," that is to say have both the
means and the freedom of action which such a force
requires (March 27, 1975). Indeed, France "must
lead the group of powers which follow the super
powers ... She is and must remain the third nuclear
super power in the world" (June 6, 1976). In so
doing, according to Giscard, France would strength-
en the effectiveness of deterrence by inducing
eventual aggressors into escalating the nature of
the conflict: "Instead of waging a conventional
war, they would be forced to take ... the risk of

nuclear war" (March 27, 1975). This was made all
the more possible given the renewed emphasis on the
extension of the national sanctuary to Europe.
"There may be," warned Giscard on February 9, 1978,
"situations in which France might feel threatened
even before her own frontiers have been reached, in
which case she would find it opportune to use her
force of dissuasion."

Yet, however independent, the French force is
a supplement to, and not a substitute for, American
protection. Thus, the withdrawal of American
troops from Europe would be "absurd" and "contrary
to the interests of the U.S. as well as to the
peaceful balance of the world," especially, one
would think, in the light of the Soviet buildup in
Central Europe. Underlying such evolution is Giscard's reassessment of the feasibility of European
defense. There, too, the early optimism soon vanished: "I think ... that Europe may assume some
day its own defense ... [Its] human and material
resources will probably enable it to organize its
defenses faster than it is believed to be possible"
(May 3, 1974). One year later (May 23, 1975), Giscard abandoned the possibility of a European defense as premature--he had by then "discovered"
the Soviet fears (a first step toward so-called
Finlandization?) and West Germany: "an essential
point is that France is opposed to any ... direct
or indirect nuclear armament of Germany." Instead,
as of 1977 the defense budget was increased--to
reach 20 percent of the overall French budget, with
a renewed emphasis on conventional forces to balance West Germany which otherwise will make, as
stated in the revealing interview of February 9,
1978, "all essential decisions in time of crisis."

As of late 1978, as it has been seen, concern
with Germany became the leitmotiv of Gaullist and
Communist criticism of the June 1979 elections of a
European parliament. By then, however, Giscard had
found his postelection domestic base to be sufficiently stable to help him balance Schmidt's economic base, at least until the time when France
would acquire "an economic force comparable to West
Germany in 1985." Hence Giscard's sponsorship, together with Schmidt, of a new relance européenne:
the confederal Europe which is being built through
the most recent European choices (Lomé II, enlargement, European parliament, and, most of all, the
European Monetary System) may well be built for a
Giscard likely to emerge by the end of his second
presidential term as a young elder statesman on the
continent.

Unlike his predecessors, Giscard also appears to be less obsessed with the primacy of the nation-state as the sole actor in international relations, the only one capable of legitimate achievements. Instead, Giscard's vision is that of a civilization moving from a "civilization of groups" to a "world-wide civilization" in which national prerogatives may be progressively relinquished in the name of so-called "ethic of deliberation" of "world-wide dimension" (May 23, 1975). Preferably, such evolution is to take place at first within the framework of Europe ("l'Europe de la nécessité," (October 26, 1974) a Europe whose "insufficient will," "lack of dynamism, and order," and resulting "slow integration" remain for a while "deplorable" (December 22-23, 1974), up to, as we have seen, the second half of 1978 when Giscard praises enthusiastically its achievements and recommends patience as even more achievements are in store for the future (since, as he professorially explains in an interview for Die Spiegel on January 1, 1979, "impatience is the enemy of the future").

Outside of Europe, this vague ethic of world-wide deliberation led Giscard to formulate a so-called policy of mondialisme, a form of diplomacie à tous les azimuts which secures the satisfaction of French interests not only in new French initiatives (disarmament, North-South, Africa) but in her participation in, and/or support of, initiatives which are most likely to provide the optimum satisfaction of France's interests (December 22-23, 1974): a mixture of concessions (the décrispation of post-Jobert relations with the U.S., or the participation to the Geneva Conference on disarmament), rhetorical adjustments (multilateralism vs. trilateralism over the North-South negotiations, or SALT vs. nuclear condominium) and well-timed, periodical visits (everywhere and from anywhere including, in early 1979, a visit to Mexico in the immediate aftermath of President Carter's trip). French efforts to promote special relationships within a bilateral framework come together with an obvious readiness to take advantage, within a multilateral framework, of any benefits which other countries might obtain. Vis a vis Iran, for instance, a special multilateral relationship with the Shah was combined, by the end of 1978, with a special bilateral relationship with the Shah's opposition, conveniently located in Paris until its return to Tehran. Such a policy is, of course, typical of France (Fourth and Fifth Republics

18

alike) that is to say, typical of a country which, in external matters, has tried (often successfully) to combine the benefits derived from national independence with those derived from various international ties and commitments. In short, what France has denied, and what it has continued and will continue to deny under Giscard, is the equation of interdependence with harmony: <u>plus ça change plus c'est la même chose</u>.

VI

The essays which follow confirm specifically what has been said before generally: America's national interest would be poorly served by the participation of the PCF in a PS-led French government.   This is not to say that such a government would engineer dramatic reversals in French foreign policy. What Giscard said on February 10, 1978 remains essentially valid: "The foreign policy of France is a topic about which there is a large enough national agreement." If it were to take place nonetheless, in however limited a fashion, a fragmentation of the existing consensus on international issues could be the work of a Chirac as easily as it could be that of a Marchais.

In any case, the major preoccupations of France are domestic: a Left in power would need to satisfy such preoccupations all the more urgently since historical precedents show how little time is given the Left to deliver on its electoral promises. The <u>Cartel des Gauches</u>, the <u>Front Populaire</u>, and the <u>Front Republicain</u> are all cases in point. Torn between its rhetorical penchant for national independence (France, Chevènement likes to say, is not a country like any other[21]) and its pragmatic assessment of international realities (France, says Mitterrand, must respect her commitments; she will be a loyal ally, even if still not an integrated one[22]), the PS will not shape a "new" foreign policy for France any more than a PCF which is itself divided between its ideological penchant for the East and its realistic acknowledgment of the West.

That their outlook should nevertheless be given careful attention is justified by three considerations. First, should political developments in 1981 confirm today's widespread predictions, the Left will nevertheless continue to draw narrow boundaries to the policies of the majority, at home and abroad. Second, today's political alliances in

19

France are too unstable to be indefinitely lasting: Giscard is probably closer to Rocard than he is to Chirac, and Marchais may paradoxically come to be closer to Chirac than he is to Mitterrand. A new defeat for the Left in 1981 may help pave the way for a reshuffling of these alliances in a Center-Left direction. Nor, finally, should a third scenario be overlooked: the Left-Right electoral division in France is--and has been for many years--so close as to make a victory of the perennial loser always possible, especially under conditions of a presidential election. In sum, while it is proper to remember that the Left failed in 1978 and reasonable to imagine that it will fail again in 1981, we may nevertheless come to see that too much was made out of 1978, and not enough of 1981--in other words, that it is the past that was imagined and the future that was remembered.

NOTES

1. For example, Jacques Chirac's statement in Le Monde, December 6, 1978. And Jacques Blanc's answer, Le Monde, February 6, 1979.
2. Alain Bournazel, La Gauche N'aura Jamais le Pouvoir (Paris: Fayolle, 1978).
3. See my own "The Fifth Republic under Giscard d'Estaing: Steadfast or Changing," The World Today, March 1975, pp. 95-103.
4. See René Chiroux, "La Fin de la Crise Constitutionelle Française?" Revue Politique et Parlementaire, September-October, 1974, pp. 21-45.
5. As analyzed by François Mitterrand in his L'Abeille et l'Architecte, Chronique (Paris: Flammarion, 1978), p. 65.
6. Neil McInnes, Euro-Communism, The Washington Papers, Vol. IV, No. 37 (Beverly Hills and London: Sage Publications, 1976), p. 16.
7. L'Abeille et l'Architecte, op.cit., p. 12.
8. Bournazel, op.cit., especially pp. 51 ff.
9. L'Abeille et l'Architecte, op.cit., p. 25.
10. Bournazel, op.cit., pp. 131-149.
11. Le Monde, March 24, 1976.
12. Le Monde, February 10, 1977, June 30, 1975, and June 18, 1976.
13. See my own "French Intellectuals and the Political Debate," The Washington Review of Strategic and International Studies, April 1978.
14. Le Monde, March 12-13, 1978.
15. L'Abeille et l'Architecte, op.cit.,

p. 373. Also, Le Monde, March 15, 1978.

16. Alexandre Adler, et.al., L'URSS et Nous (Paris: Editions Sociales, 1978), passim.

17. Le Monde, December 12, 1978.

18. See his Politique (Paris: Fayard, 1977).

19. See Rocard's interview in Le Nouvel Observateur, October 2, 1978. See also the same publication dated December 30, 1978. A useful comparison of the various PS tendencies is found in Le Monde, February 16, 1979.

20. John C. Cairns, "France, Europe, and the 'Design of the World,'" International Journal, Spring 1977, pp. 253-271.

21. Parti Socialiste, Socialisme et Multinationales (Paris: Flammarion, 1976), p. 179 (1976 colloquium of the Paris Federation).

22. Le Monde, January 10, 1978.

2
The Socialist Party, the Union of the Left, and French National Security

Michael M. Harrison

In the wake of a narrow but frustrating electoral defeat in 1978, the French Union of the Left
appears to have collapsed for the foreseeable future while open warfare has broken out within a
Socialist Party intent on reassessing its past programs, commitments, and leadership. Security and
defense policies, however, are least affected by
the volatility and uncertainty of such circumstances. For one, both parties developed their defense and alliance perspectives out of the Gaullist
paradigm of independence, which has attained the
status of a broad national consensus and sets the
terms and parameters of French debates over these
issues. Although the Gaullist model is flexible
and allows enough latitude for shifts in policies
according to domestic and international conditions,
it does impose a legacy that constrains the choices
of government and opposition alike. In addition,
areas of agreement and disagreement were fairly
well defined and thrashed out between the Socialists and the Communists during the years 1972-1978:
thus riddled with contradictions, security policy
did not become a major bone of contention as the
Union of the Left floundered and finally broke down
after mid-1977.

SECURITY AND A PLURALIST LEFT IN FRANCE

Despite their superficial reconciliation on
defense issues, the leftist partners have been generally unable to disguise often incompatible views
and interests that have divided party factions as
well as the interparty alliance. Thus, a gradual
adaptation to de Gaulle's defense policy has been
difficult and awkward for a left long accustomed to

simplistic criticism and posturing that usually betray an unwillingness to confront its own confused priorities. Socialists and Communists alike have been unable to overcome fully their own ineptitude in handling security issues, and have thereby reinforced widespread doubts about the maturity, competence, and intentions of leftist parties and elites with claims to national power. Such problems have often surfaced to reveal starkly divergent perspectives on France's international role, her alignments, and her status within an interdependent Western capitalist order. For those on the left, the most profound aspect of the debate involved the penalties of entanglement within an American- and German-dominated Western system, and the costs or benefits of minimizing such restraints on the ambitious architects of a new socialist order in France. Intraleft disagreement, then, has essentially focused on different estimates of the need to make international compromises and concessions in order to manage external restraints and gain maximum leverage and leeway to pursue socialist goals. Debate over security policy in France is always heated because the issue has such a high symbolic value for French elites, but in this case it has inevitably been linked to a dramatic and controversial leftist challenge to both the domestic status quo and France's general attachment to the Western capitalist system.

The Left's congenital inability to establish its own priorities has doubtless been exacerbated by interparty divisions and sometimes radical fluctuations in Socialist and Communist assessments of the domestic and international situations. Abrupt shifts in the views of the French Communist Party (PCF) may reflect uncertainties inherent in a recent independence within the international communist movement, and an inability to find a comfortable relationship with the Soviet Union that is also compatible with the shifting priorities of national communism. Despite its awkward handling of many issues, in defense affairs the PCF does seem to be guided by a consistent antagonism towards French association with Atlantic or West European security institutions--a stand that is perfectly compatible with general communist hostility to economic and political dependence on the West. Because the Communists often cannot directly attack all the instruments of Western capitalist interdependence, they have sometimes focused on defense and security issues as a metaphorical arena for exposing the

23

party's own international choices. The particular
French Communist ideological paradigm and habit of
relying on Soviet analyses of the international
situation often leads the PCF to embrace Soviet security perspectives, even when they seem to be at
odds with the party's recent commitment to defining
its own domestic and international priorities.

Although Communists and Socialists have both
provided evidence of ill-defined or contradictory
perspectives on West European security in the context of East-West détente, the Socialist Party (Parti socialiste, or PS) has faced the distinctive
problem of managing diverse and often combative factions within its organization. Thus it has been
difficult for PS elites to produce coherent policy
because, on defense and most other issues, the party
is awash with different viewpoints and postures
that only sometimes coincide with the "official"
majority-minority division that emerged after the
new party was formed in 1971.[1] François Mitterrand's leadership has doubtless compounded this
particular problem, because he has held the party
and, until recently, the Left together through a
cultivated talent for ambiguity, indecision, vacil-
lation, and dissimulation. In security matters, at
any rate, Mitterrand often appears to be uncertain
of his own attitudes and interests, and this state
of mind has only stimulated the contradictions that
characterize Socialist Party policy.

ELUSIVE THREATS AND HOSTILE ALLIES

The stormy alliance between Socialists and Communists in France was based on the Socialist Party's
post-1971 commitment to an anticapitalist philos-
ophy assigning priority attention to socio-economic
factors of domestic and international politics.
Socialist security perspectives shifted closer to
a communist framework as traditional diplomatic and
military interpretations of international threats
were superceded (but not entirely replaced) by a
neo-Marxist analysis asserting that the structure
of international politics is primarily a product of
economic relations and the international division
of labor. Estimates of political-military intentions were inevitably accorded less weight in this
analysis than factors of political economy that determine imperialist activities and the structure of
international dominance and dependence.[2] Given
their values and this analytical framework,

24

Socialist elites could more easily sympathize with Communist sensitivities to the potential costs of international economic interdependence and the severe restraints it might impose on an audacious domestic program deemed incompatible with the structure and logic of the Western system. The principal threats to French independence, especially under a hypothetical leftist regime, were identified as international capitalist financial and market instruments acting in alliance with the strongest capitalist powers, the United States and West Germany. This situation posed an awkward dilemma for PS security policy, because the actions most hostile to a socialist France were expected to emerge in the context of relations with ostensible partners and allies--and were actually in contradiction with the formal structure of international political-military alliances and confrontations. Hence both Socialists and Communists often identified the United States as a dominant global power raising a variety of real and potential risks to French interests, particularly as a future source of sabotage against a socialist socio-economic order.

Most postwar French governments have been exceedingly wary of the costs of dependence on an American-dominated West, and have sought to limit the restraints and piece together maximum leeway and independence. But the Left certainly ascribed a more pervasive and insidious hostility to France's close allies than these governments, including even de Gaulle at the brief zenith of his policy of independence and grandeur from 1966-1968. This perspective was a prominent feature of the new PS until perhaps 1975. Profound Communist distrust of the Socialists' intentions and commitments were overcome or set aside in 1972 partly because the PS's international perspective seemed radical enough to give grounds for hope that the minimalist Common Program could be transformed into a maximalist Communist strategy of rupture with the West.[3] Within the PS, the extremist and anti-Atlanticist views of the CERES groups were particularly influential until 1975 and lent support to Communist expectations. It is difficult to determine precisely when Socialist Party views began to shift away from this pervasive antagonism towards France's major Western partners. The influence of CERES over party policy declined after the Congress of Pau in February 1975, when the abrasive minority was barred from positions on the Secretariat and Mitterrand's own pragmatic cadres and their more moderate allies

25

began consolidating their domination. A number of
other factors doubtless contributed to a partial
moderation of PS views and an estrangement from the
more inflexible Communist position. They include:
the new influence of anticommunist elements such
as Michel Rocard and Christian militants after
1975, the failure of radical experiments in Portugal, the accommodation of the Italian Communist
Party to Western economic and security institutions,
a declining American interest in overt or covert
intervention abroad, the growing strength and con-
fidence of the PS itself, and the party's closer
ties with other European socialists (especially the
reformist SPD) in the context of the Socialist
International.

Perhaps the most significant Socialist-Communist divergence arose over assessments of the international economic crisis and a preferred leftist
strategy for coping with its effects on France. The
Communists continued to rely essentially on their
"socialism in one country" perspective, which
stressed a rupture with some key international capitalist restraints and rigid control of others by a
centralized, state-dominated socialist system.[4] On
the other hand, with some strong dissent from
CERES, the majority of the PS shifted towards a mix-
ed national and international solution while it retained the party's commitment to the autogestion
socio-economic model that seems to be the antithesis
of PCF ideals. By 1977, PS international policy was
based on the assumption that a Socialist-dominated
left government in France could secure the international concessions necessary for a domestic transition to socialism. Thus it could avoid the drastic
ruptures judged by most to be dangerous and counter-
productive in a period of serious economic disrup-
tion and decay. In the PS, then, there was evidence of a new moderation and unwillingness to expand the scope of the Common Program at the risk of
economic chaos and a forced retreat to the national
autarky favored by the Communists. Finally, just as
the Communists' preference for national economic
self-reliance was accompanied by a stress on defense
autonomy compatible with relative isolation from the
West, the Socialist refusal to countenance a rupture
with the Western international economy was comple-
mented by a stronger insistence on maintaining basic
French ties to the Western allies and avoiding moves
in any sphere which could jeopardize a fragile Western system.

In a decade dominated by economic issues--

national and international, actual and hypotheti-
cal--military threats have not usually preoccupied
left leaders. A focus on the inconveniences of
Western economic interdependence did, however,
sometimes evoke public discussion of military in-
terventions or pressures from France's ostensible
allies. The possibility of this kind of American
(or West German) action was usually mentioned in
the context of the Chilean misadventure and a capitalist repertory of subversion, destabilization,
and intimidation.[5] Socialist Party defense experts
cited an independent national defense as the best
guarantee against such measures, and the argument
did sometimes extend to indulgent speculation about
how to ward off American or West German armed
forces.[6] For the PCF, there has never been any
doubt whatsoever that the only significant imperialist threats to France emanate from the United
States and West Germany, the latter having become
"the heir to German militarism."[7]

On the other hand, until the 1977 rupture of
the left alliance, the issue of a Soviet political-
military threat to France and Western Europe was
treated gingerly by Socialist Party leaders. This
was partly in deference to Communist sensitivities;
it was also a consequence of Socialist preoccupa-
tion with instruments of economic intervention that
naturally diverted attention from the East. Thus
the dominant opinion in the PS seemed to be that
the Soviet Union was essentially a defensive state,
compensating for an inefficient economic system by
building up exaggerated military power in Europe
and on the seas.[8] The left wing of the PS was especially determined that the specter of Soviet military imperialism should not again be manipulated to
divert the Socialists from their ideological goals
and induce them to compromise with Western capitalism. As long as the Union of the Left was intact,
the PS also had an intrinsic interest in minimizing
East-West tensions that might jeopardize a détente
environment conducive to the political success of
the left in France and elsewhere, and constituting
a broad but important condition for the Socialist-
Communist alliance itself.

This perspective changed somewhat as a result
of tensions within the Union of the Left, and a generally cloudy atmosphere of East-West détente in
light of Soviet internal repression and the remark-
able expansion of Soviet military power. By 1977,
then, the Socialist Party had become more sensitive
to the arguments of its own right wing, particularly

27

of Robert Pontillon, the Secretariat's expert on
international affairs, who had long insisted that
Soviet inability to use sophisticated political-
economic instruments of hegemony made crude military
power a more attractive weapon for Soviet leaders.[9]
By November 1977, the PS bureau exécutif was able
to agree on a defense platform singling out the
U.S.S.R. as the only power to conduct military actions in Europe since the end of World War II,
against Hungary and Czechoslovakia. This was given
as the principal reason for continuing to adhere to
the Atlantic Alliance, a rationale bound to antag-
onize the French Communists. While PCF relations
with Moscow had deteriorated significantly by this
time, Communist Party leaders still seemed unable
to imagine a Soviet threat to a democratic and socialist France, nor could they easily contemplate
the use of military force or even instruments of
deterrence against the homeland of the communist
revolution.

These divergent perspectives emerged most
clearly in debates over French nuclear strategy,
but they were also readily apparent in different
and often fluctuating Socialist and Communist approaches to France's formal alliance commitments,
and especially the Atlantic Alliance. After abandoning the SFIO's basically pro-NATO views of the
1960s, the new Socialist Party originally adopted
the position of its young radicals and Mitterrand's
ambitious cadres, who asserted that "For France,
membership in the bloc of the Atlantic Alliance does
not signify a guarantee of security, but offers an
additional facility for her economic colonization
by the United States."[10] Thus the Socialist Party
program of 1972 accepted the Gaullist solution to
Alliance membership and did not urge an outright
withdrawal, pending the simultaneous dissolution of
both military blocs. It did, however, note that
membership was still a substantial inconvenience because the Atlantic Treaty "ties all signatories to
American imperialism and in the case of war involving the United States exposes them to preventive
attacks."[11] When it came time to negotiate the
Common Program with the Communists, the reluctant
pragmatism of the PS prevailed over the Communist
stand in favor of a full withdrawal from the Alliance. This major Communist concession was con-
cealed in a vague statement that committed a government of the united left to "respect for France's
existing alliances."[12] Greater emphasis was placed,
however, on a left government's determination to

pursue a resolutely independent policy toward all political-military blocs, and to work for a European collective security system that would render such alliances obsolete.

After the ascendancy of moderates within the PS, the party convention in January 1978 reaffirmed the commitment to the Atlantic Alliance in more positive terms and seemed to offer it as a guarantee against irresponsible leftist ruptures with the Western international order. Thus the Socialists rejected the persistent Communist preference for "la France seule" and asserted that in the event of a clear aggression against her allies, a socialist France would fulfill her obligations under both the Brussels and Atlantic treaties.[13] Reflecting a new enthusiasm for the Atlantic security connection, Mitterrand cited approvingly the Gaullist precedent of maintaining basic Atlantic ties and even insisted that "the Americans ought to know that we will be loyal allies, if there is a war and if this war is provoked by the desires of outside powers."[14] Such warmer accommodation to the Atlantic Alliance was doubtless prompted by a recent inclination to avoid unnecessary international confrontations, particularly during a vulnerable transition to socialism under a hypothetical left regime. Another factor favoring "detachment without disengagement"[15] is the flexible kind of Alliance membership de Gaulle carved out for France after 1966--one that permits closer or more distant political-military relations with the United States and NATO according to both government composition and the course of substantive disagreements over issues. Charles Hernu, the leading PS defense expert, has commented favorably on the NATO trend towards a looser structure, noting that allied governments can now engage in dialogues over security issues without facing the constant threat of submission to an American-dominated military structure.[16] Others in the party, however, might object that a network of bilateral European ties with the United States is unlikely to be very constructive in the long run. In particular, it probably could not stimulate the European unity seen by some Socialists as a preferable alternative to a looser Western system that still leaves the United States as the dominant military power.

Despite a more favorable position on the Western Alliance, the Socialist Party has constantly reaffirmed its anti-Atlanticist and Gaullist credentials by resolutely opposing any form of French reintegration into the NATO military structure that might compromise the independence of France's defense system. Thus the PS has been careful to rely on the Gaullist precept that France must retain her essential autonomy of decision in military affairs, to avoid being dragged into a conflict where French interests or responsibilities are not at stake. This stand is not surprising, because no French political leader of importance directly challenges the withdrawal from NATO integration, although Giscard d'Estaing's Atlanticist tendencies have made him vulnerable on this issue and subject to frequent attacks by Communists, Socialists, and ardent Gaullists.

While the leftist parties have been able to sustain agreement on the issue of NATO integration, it does seem that their original pact in favor of Alliance membership was tainted by Communist reservations that tended to invalidate the 1972 agreement in the Common Program. According to Georges Marchais' report to the Central Committee on June 27, 1972, the PCF had not really revised its basic judgment that the Atlantic Alliance (and the EEC) was a vehicle for "imprisoning our country in the imperialist system under the direction of the United States." It was, he said, a fundamental Communist goal to use both foreign and military policy to liberate France from "the class imperatives of the world imperialist system," adding that the Common Program should be seen as a first step in fulfilling the PCF aim of gradual French disengagement from the Atlantic Alliance.[17] After the signing of the Common Program, the Communist Party did not lose an opportunity to bemoan the alliance provisions and to suggest that French interests would be served by renegotiating the Atlantic Treaty's provisions as they apply to France, in order to minimize all contacts with Western allies.[18]

For some time, Socialists and Communists did manage to paper over their basic disagreement on the Alliance issue by their common commitment to work for the eventual dissolution of both military blocs. This perspective was compatible with traditional French hostility to a bipolar order that limits the independence of middle-range powers and subjects all states to the twin dangers of superpower conflict or condominium. As noted previously, Socialist leaders and programs often resorted to exhortations for France to combat the hegemonic tendencies of the superpowers and work for the disappearance of the blocs.[19] Reflecting the strong

30

Gaullist influence on their thinking, the Socialists' long-range and largely rhetorical goal was to
secure national independence from both military systems and encourage the evolution of a more pluralist international framework. Despite a superficial
agreement on this perspective, it seems that the
Communists went much further than the Socialists
and interpreted their bloc position as a tactic for
chipping away at French alignment with the West
while establishing new and eventually decisive ties
to the East and the radical Third World. The 1972
Marchais report, for example, cited the Communist
Party's policy of "independence towards any political-military bloc" as simply another version of the
Communist position on disengagement from the Atlantic Alliance.[20] Marchais and the party apparently
still adhered to this strategy in March 1978, when
the Secretary-General insisted that "France ought
to practice a policy founded on the rejection of
alignment--of any alignment with anyone whatsoever."[21] During the 1977 negotiations on updating
the Common Program, the Communists proposed a non-
alignment policy involving treaties of nonaggression and renunciation of force with the East, a
move that Mitterrand and the PS rejected outright
because it implied the sanctioning of a neutral
status for France.[22]

The Communists have been able to include a
perspective of neutrality within the Gaullist security model, because of the "tous azimuts" position adopted by de Gaulle for a brief time at the
end of 1967. But neutrality and a more drastic reversal of alliances was not part of de Gaulle's
security repertory, even though by the mid-1960s he
may have perceived the need to combat a nascent
American global hegemony by offering some support
to the Soviet Union and the Third World. De
Gaulle's most characteristic formula for an ambitious transformation of the international system
involved the construction of a French-led European
bloc, united and independent of the superpowers.
The left has been unable to agree on this point.
The Communists are fundamentally opposed to any
West European cooperation with a political or military dimension, and suspicion of Socialist Party
toleration for some future EDC evidently contributed
to Communist intransigence during the 1977 Common
Program negotiations.[23] There is indeed a pro-
European bias within the Socialist Party, where
the majority has emphasized a formal PS commitment
to European unity and some figures can even envisage

a military dimension to this cooperation.[24] The
party's left flank, grouped around CERES, has resisted this commitment because it sees that the
Community is unlikely to foster socialist goals,
may in fact sabotage a socialist program in France,
and is incapable of becoming an economic or political-military counterweight to the United States.
Hence Jean-Pierre Chevènement and his allies have
implicitly argued that the left government in
France cannot expect to construct an international
alternative to the bloc system, and should tempo-
rarily secede from it alone and adopt a posture of
semiautonomy resembling the Communist model.[25]
Perhaps the only conclusion one can draw from these
diverse and contradictory attitudes is that the
Socialist Party, at least, has no grand alternative
to propose to the contemporary international security structure--other than somewhat worn rhetoric
about how an avant-garde socialist France is bound
to serve as a stimulus for transforming the international system. For its part, the PCF's recent
commitment to a democratic and pluralistic political
system for France, and its apparent adherence to
the Italian Communist perspective on a pluralistic
international communist system, have evidently not
led the party to make the same kinds of pragmatic
accommodations and commitments to France's Atlantic
and European roles.

NUCLEAR WEAPONS AND DETERRENCE

    De Gaulle's most concrete legacy and guarantee
of French independence has been the force nucléaire
stratégique. Whereas the status of the most visible
symbol of France's grandeur was once likely to be
jeopardized by a left regime, this no longer seems
to be the case due to shifts in perspective on the
part of the major left-wing parties. This is an
important change of attitude for both Communists
and Socialists, who had previously condemned national nuclear forces and threatened at different times
to dismantle the French one, renounce it, or at
least not promote its development. In 1965, for
example, Mitterrand's presidential program condemned the notion that France could have a full defense
system of her own, particularly one based on a small
nuclear force that was "ineffectual, costly, and
dangerous." The force, he said categorically,
should be dismantled.[26] By 1972, however, the program of the radicalized Socialist Party had become

more ambiguous--it mentioned "renouncing" the nuclear force along with a "reconversion of atomic
industry," but the only genuine commitment was to
"interrupt the construction of the force de frappe"
by halting atmospheric nuclear tests.[27] Socialist
reservations about the wisdom of immediately jetti-
soning France's nuclear deterrent system nearly
broke up negotiations with the Communists on the
Common Program that same year, until a compromise
was reached in which the nuclear force was to be
"renounced" and all construction halted, but no
precise schedule or commitment to dismantle was
made. By 1974, the united left's position had become sufficiently muddled for Mitterrand to state
that although his first priority was not to promote
the development of the nuclear force he had no intention of liquidating existing armaments without
international guarantees.[28] These subtle and gla-
cial changes in Socialist attitudes were the result of patient work by Charles Hernu and his group
of defense experts. Since 1971 this group had been
urging Mitterrand and the party leadership to accept at least a "minimum deterrent force" as protection against unknown future threats, and particularly "to ward off any risk of aggression against
the construction of a socialist society as long as
the blocs have not disarmed."[29] Hernu's position
gradually gained acceptance among the elite, so
that by November 1976 a discussion at a meeting of
the Comité directeur seemed to reflect a consensus
that the nuclear force is indeed an indispensable
means of protecting the independence of a socialist
France.[30]
     The evolution in Socialist thinking was also
characteristic of the Communist Party, which abandoned its once-fervent opposition to French nuclear
weapons. Envisaged by some Communist defense experts since at least early 1976,[31] the somewhat
abrupt change in policy came in May 1977 in the
form of a report to the Central Committee. It was
presented by Jean Kanapa and argued that only the
nuclear deterrent protects France against external
aggression, due to the weakness of her conventional
forces.[32] After long and abrasive criticism of the
FNS, the Communist rally seemed to stem from a realization that these weapons could be useful in
convincing the Socialists to sever ties with NATO
military organs and redirect France's entire defense system away from its preferred targeting on
the Soviet Union. Both Socialists and Communists
must also have perceived that public accommodation

33

to the FNS was a politically astute means of placating and even seducing a French bourgeoisie attracted to Gaullist symbols of independence. It
could also reassure the most sophisticated and
technologically oriented military cadres that the
foundation of France's defense network would not be
summarily discarded by a leftist regime.

Many of the advantages of the new position
were, however, undermined by the left's inability
to come to terms honestly and directly with the conclusions and recommendations of its own experts.
The Socialist Party bore great responsibility,
partly because François Mitterrand continued to be
troubled by a profound moral reservation about nuclear weapons that reinforced his natural political
prudence. It is also true that Socialist Party
militants have strong pacifist, antimilitarist,
and antinuclear sentiments that became increasingly vocal and complicated decision making for party
elites.[33] These factors played a prominent role in
the 1977 renegotiation of the Common Program, in
which the parties at times seemed able to agree to
maintain the FNS in working order pending the outcome of a major French initiative in favor of general nuclear disarmament. The Socialist Party, however, could not take a definitive position and fed
Communist suspicions by insisting that a clear commitment would have to await a Socialist convention
on defense scheduled for late 1977. In the end,
Mitterrand's last-minute proposal for an eventual
referendum on the nuclear force was interpreted as
yet another example of PS indecision and evasion,
as it confirmed Communist fears that the PS would
be an unreliable government partner, constantly in-
clined to outflank or undermine the Common Program
and the PCF with Gaullist-type public appeals.[34]
A relatively minor issue in relation to the FNS itself, the ill-considered referendum idea evidently
made an important contribution to the breakdown of
the leftist alliance by the fall of 1977.

All along, the Communists understandably
deplored leaving the Union of the Left's policy on
such an important issue up in the air until the
PS could sort out its internal disagreements on nuclear weapons. Yet, Socialist discussions continued
to betray a rather uncertain commitment to the FNS
and the principle of national deterrence. On the
one hand, the CERES position resembled that of the
PCF and insisted on firm support for the strategic
force as a basis for relative autonomy from the
United States. But a strong antinuclear element

in the party, which cut across the major factions, resisted an unqualified commitment and insisted that at least the national territory be denuclearized by relying solely on the submarine part of the deterrent. This group remained quite hostile to even the concept of an independent nuclear force and seemed to prefer a stronger French dependence on the Atlantic Alliance and the American nuclear guarantee.[35] Mitterrand himself, while criticizing the CERES position, and sometimes seeming to be partial to the antinuclear arguments, did nevertheless support a basic decision in favor of maintaining the FNS pending the outcome of a major Socialist campaign in favor of international disarmament. Approved by the party national convention in January 1978, this reversal of previous Socialist positions finally brought the Left around to a minimum consensus on the nuclear issue.[36]

Leftist mores require that such a radical departure from the ideological aversion to nuclear weapons be presented as a temporary aberration until the world comes to its senses and agrees to a general disarmament program which will induce all states to abandon their arsenals. Communist and Socialist elites are perhaps genuinely committed to this viewpoint, which has also helped them justify their new policies to suspicious and even hostile militant opinion. Thus the Socialist Party could "solemnly" announce "that it is ready to renounce nuclear arms" and seek "a world conference on disarmament or, failing that, a conference of nuclear powers."[37] Among the other measures proposed by the Socialists were severe restraints on French arms sales, measures against the dissemination of nuclear technology, termination of the French nuclear testing program, and French participation in existing arms control forums such as the Geneva and MBFR talks. Although there were differences between particular Communist and Socialist positions, a strong mutual interest in this theme has been perhaps the most coherent element of left defense policy and naturally received priority attention by both parties.[38]

Although the French Left was able to achieve a certain consensus on arms control and disarmament because of its characteristic addiction to utopian projects, on more practical and immediate issues such as the structure and strategic orientation of French national defense, Communists and Socialists have had trouble finding a basis for agreement or eventual government policy. Thus, the PS

35

Commission on National Defense had indicated a preference for modernizing the submarine fleet and furnishing it with an independent satellite alert system in place of the present dependence on the NATO
network.[39] In January 1978, the party agreed that a
left government would "renounce" the Mirage force
and consider abandoning the land-based missiles if
there were any significant developments in reciprocal disarmament projects. The Socialist decision to
give up the Mirage component of the FNS was singled
out by Mitterrand as an example of the party's willingness even to engage in "a form of unilateral disarmament" and induce other powers to follow the
French example.[40] Mitterrand did, nevertheless, insist that the party "will not destroy the atomic arsenal and, by maintaining it intact, and not only
intact, we will carry out the technical modifications required by the advance or progress of technology..."[41] For its part, the PCF Central Committee accepted the full French triad and also urged
technological innovations such as satellite and air-
borne radar systems.[42] During negotiations with the
Socialists in 1977, the PCF argued for the goal of
full independence from NATO detection systems, while
the Socialists maintained that, for the time being,
the situation was one of reciprocal dependence that
would not interfere with the autonomy of French military decisions in a crisis.[43] The discussions did,
however, seem to indicate agreement on eventually
finding a means of independent warning against
aggression.
    The complexities of finding a nuclear deter-
rence strategy for a left-wing medium-sized power
raised one of the most vexing problems for the Union
of the Left, not so much because of technical issues
of appropriate weapons systems and targeting requirements,[44] but because of the political implications of a particular strategic emphasis. Left
parties may, however, find some comfort in the fact
that there is ample precedent for contradiction,
confusion, and inspired ambiguity in strategic
thinking under the Fifth Republic--even though a
certain degree of evasion is justified in deterrence strategy and has probably enhanced the value
of the FNS. Gaullist doctrine essentially rested
on the argument that a small, independent nuclear
force was a valid proportional deterrent against
attack by larger powers when it could pose the
threat of retaliating and causing "unacceptable
damage" to the aggressor. It was never entirely
clear if de Gaulle accepted the extreme argument of

General Gallois that such a threat was sufficient in itself, without the additional menace that the smaller power might trigger a nuclear exchange between superpowers because of the alliance system. The latter view, developed by General Beaufre under the rubric of multilateral deterrence, would seem to have been the actual strategic doctrine of de Gaulle's regime and its successors, because they have all depended for security on both the FNS and Atlantic Alliance ties to the American strategic force. One can also maintain that the existence of a semiautonomous French nuclear force has enhanced the over-all security of Western Europe, because it serves as an additional factor of uncertainty and risk in the context of European theater deterrence.

Apart from its function as a potential trigger that reinforces theater deterrence on behalf of Western Europe, Gaullist doctrine has also emphasized the force's utility as a vehicle of neutrality in the sense of enabling a French government to decide to remain apart from an armed conflict if the national interest were not engaged. It was the need to preserve a maximum freedom of decision in such cases that preoccupied de Gaulle most and led him to disengage from NATO as well as to build a nuclear force. This was the more nationalistic aspect of French strategic thinking and it led to the short-lived Ailleret notion of a "tous azimuts" defense in 1967-1968, in which French neutrality may have been conceived in the framework of a global nuclear deterrent and full political independence from the Atlantic Alliance and European allies. No practical measures were taken to fill in the outlines of the doctrine, however.

Finally, mention should be made of the Gaullist approach to the American flexible response strategy of reserving strategic nuclear forces for a late entry in the course of conventional and theater nuclear battles in Europe. This position was modified slightly by the introduction of tactical nuclear weapons into the French armory, and by 1969, French Chief of Staff Fourquet could conceive of French participation in tactical nuclear engagements along German approaches to the French frontier, in order to test the intentions of an enemy to cross that frontier and trigger the strategic force. This conception of "two battles" involving French security, a first one in Germany engaging French forces only under certain conditions, and a second one on the national territory

37

automatically triggering the FNS, was perhaps the
bitterest aspect of French defense policy as far as
West European cooperation was concerned.

A summary explanation of Gaullist strategic
views has been necessary because Socialist and Communist thinking on such issues is largely derived
from these concepts, emphasizing one or the other
as is most convenient for the broad political and
security goals of the party. Recourse to often
narrow interpretations of Gaullist security policy
has also been useful fodder for attacks on Giscard
d'Estaing's modifications in this field, which de-
emphasize a rigid national deterrence in favor of
defense collaboration with Atlantic allies. The
principal concern of the Socialists seemed to be to
return to a posture of absolute deterrence, elimin-
ating plans for preliminary engagements of non-
strategic forces and restoring the FNS role of en-
suring that a European conflict involving France
would escalate rapidly. The corollary Gaullist
theory was also stressed, namely, that the FNS may
serve to protect France against unwilling involvement in a European conflict because "it is an arm
of neutrality."[45] This position was reconcilable
with previous defense policy. Nevertheless, the
concept of neutrality was flexible enough to set
the stage for a shift from merely preserving a
capacity for noninvolvement in a crisis, to a more
ominous political definition of armed neutrality
sometimes attributed to the Ailleret strategy of
"tous azimuts."

This issue blossomed during 1977 and contributed to the escalation of conflict between Socialists and Communists. For the PCF interpreted the
Common Program agreement on military strategy,
which mentioned a capacity "to oppose any aggressor
whatsoever," as the equivalent of a neutral position with no predesignated enemy or target. The
Communists were essentially pursuing their interest in adjusting targeting plans and strategy away
from the Soviet bloc, while the Socialists proved
unwilling to jeopardize the Atlantic Alliance tie
by giving the West "equal time" along these lines.
As Mitterrand said, he did "not perceive the necessity of pointing our missiles at our own allies."[46]
Although it revealed significant differences in the
bloc perspectives and alliance interests of the
leftist parties, the argument ended inconclusively
in a mutual willingness to consider the feasibility
of abandoning all predesignated targeting for the
nuclear force.[47] The Socialists later seemed

unwilling to go even this far, probably because a
truly neutral FNS in the hands of a left government seems incompatible with membership in the Atlantic Alliance, which, by its nature, commits allies to a priority military engagement against the
Warsaw Pact. In general, it seems that the French
Left's internal contradictions and indecision
would have undermined the credibility of a small
nuclear deterrent. As if to confirm such an assessment, the Left insisted on raising the rather
artificial and demagogic issue of how to control
the triggering of the nuclear force. Of course,
both Communists and Socialists have often insisted
on restoring parliamentary and cabinet influence
over an imperial or arbitrary presidential office
and, specifically, they have refuted the Gaullist
notion of a "domaine réservé" in defense affairs.
In addition to a greater parliamentary and cabinet
role in the making of defense policy, the Left began to insist that an exclusive presidential decision to trigger the FNS was ideologically distaste-
ful and perhaps dangerous. The Communists proposed
that any decision be made instead by a National Defense Committee, composed of the president, prime
minister, chief of the general staff, and other
members approved by parliament--although the president was to retain responsibility for executing the
decision.[48] Despite some typical and tiresome
quarreling over vocabulary and intentions, the
Socialists could only agree that the FNS should be
subject to broader, more stringent, and more democratic controls than has been the case in the past.

THE NATIONAL SANCTUARY AND EUROPEAN DEFENSE

     A related dilemma for the Left has been
France's strategic ties to her European neighbors
and, by implication, to the NATO system that would
direct the course of a conflict on the Central
Front. The issue has become prominent recently because of changes in government policy that favor
an early French participation in the forward "battle of Germany," to be fought along NATO guidelines stressing conventional defense and relatively
late escalation to selective use of tactical nuclear weapons. The new French position was an-
nounced in the spring of 1976 after long presidential reflection under the influence of the current
Chief of the General Staff, Army General G. Méry.
The latter has described his position in favor of

39

the concept of an "enlarged sanctuary" around
France, where conventional defense forces would be
capable of intervening in crises and military conflicts.[49] According to Giscard d'Estaing, the government no longer assumes the existence of two distinct security zones in Europe as far as France is
concerned. In the event of a conflict, the president has stated, "... there will be only one space,
and the French space will from the beginning be in
the zone of a battle which will be general."[50] As
a consequence of this new perspective, although the
ultimate French freedom of decision to participate
or not is still formally intact, it can be assumed
that NATO contingency plans based on French participation have been upgraded and expanded on the
assumption of closer collaboration in terms of
tactical battle plans.

Even in the absence of more detailed informa-
tion or precise knowledge of the Ailleret-Lemnitzer
Agreements on French-NATO military cooperation, it
would seem that the present government has gone far
beyond its predecessors in terms of strategic theory. The Méry-Giscard doctrine cannot be considered
a simple extension of previous plans for French
actions beyond the frontier in Germany, because
guidelines developed under de Gaulle and Pompidou
restricted such actions to brief, small-scale engagements, perhaps involving tactical nuclear weapons and intended primarily to avoid a premature
firing of the strategic nuclear force itself. Recent plans do not appear to be directly linked to
the FNS, whereas they do bring over-all French defense strategy more in line with American flexible
response guidelines for European defense. Apart
from closer French coordination with allied contingency plans, however, it is difficult to see what
practical measures have been taken to implement and
solidify the new French alignment with NATO. For,
instead of beefing up French forces in or near Germany, the government has actually reduced them in
line with a program of creating smaller, more mo-
bile divisions and dispersing them more widely over
French territory. Thus Giscard's rapprochement to
NATO has not borne obvious military benefits in
terms of ready forces on the central front, although the creation of more modern and battle-
ready French combat units is a favorable development from NATO's point of view. On the other hand,
one consequence of a new French emphasis on conventional defense may be an unfortunate devaluation
of the French contribution to the multilateral

nuclear deterrence in Europe, which was the fruit
of France's unique position as an independent ally
armed with credible strategic weapons and not subject to American strategic doctrines.

The left has certainly been troubled by the
prospect of French collaboration in large-scale
conventional and tactical nuclear warfare (TNW) in
Europe, a possibility that grows stronger with any
French accommodation to NATO flexible response
plans. The TNW issue is a particularly sensitive
one because almost any plans for their use are
bound to extend the escalation process, detract
from absolute national deterrence, and involve
France in allied defense plans. The Giscard-Méry
strategy alters previous guidelines by seeming to
stress TNW utility as "an instrument of battle" as
well as one of deterrence, so that the Pluton's
function as a trigger for the FNS is now less prominent than in the past.[51] France has not, however,
developed coherent and precise plans for using her
TNWs, any more than NATO has for its American-
controlled weapons. The French position remains
particularly ambiguous because the Pluton is to be
used only on German territory, yet Paris will not
relinquish national control over the weapons so the
Pluton regiments have had to remain in France.

Whatever their current status, the propensity
of the army's tactical arms to engage France in
European defense cooperation, and in the controversial "forward battle," has made the Left extremely reserved and pessimistic about this weapon's future utility to a socialist government. The
Communists have naturally insisted that the TNWs
remain on national territory and uncoordinated with
NATO planning. Socialist Charles Hernu has branded
the Pluton a "dangerous toy" of desanctuarization
that could turn Europe into a nuclear battle-
field.[52] At their 1978 convention on defense policy, however, the Socialists seemed unable to arrive
at a clear position on this question. Despite an
insistence on maintaining the Gaullist heritage of
defense autonomy and absolute deterrence,[53] the
party rejected amendments warning France against a
"harmonization of her strategy with that of the
United States in Europe."[54] Given the confusion
that has surrounded recent leftist defense debates,
it is impossible to say whether or not such actions
indicate an actual PS shift in favor of forward defense and more European military cooperation, in
the context of the Franco-German alliance.

CONCLUSION

This analysis has suggested that the thrust of
leftist defense and security policy in France has
been to adapt to the Gaullist model established
under the Fifth Republic. For both the Socialists
and the Communists, it is clear that the cornucopia
of Gaullist policies and postures furnishes ample
material to suit the often divergent and clashing
interests of the various actors. Intraleft disagreements on defense do reflect contradictory
goals or interpretations of domestic and international issues, but it is revealing that explana-
tions or justifications have increasingly resorted
to the Gaullist security model as a guideline or
natural point of reference.

The Left's embrace of Fifth Republic security
policy is not surprising, because in this arena de
Gaulle represented attitudes and views widely shared by French elites and generally appealing to the
nation as a whole. France's leadership, as well as
the political opposition, have also been concerned
with the consequences of international economic
interdependence, and the Left has seized on the
Gaullist defense legacy as one tool among others
for limiting and managing the many constraints of
the international system. This is certainly in accord with the intentions of de Gaulle. On the
other hand, while the search for independence in
the 1960s entailed a certain autonomy and distance
from the American-dominated Western security system, this autonomy was always partial and carefully
controlled to avoid irresponsible damage to the
West or France's own interests. Nor was the Gaullist challenge distorted and exaggerated by ideological attachment to an alternative model of socio-
economic organization on the domestic or international levels. In many respects, the French Left
has offered this kind of challenge and has therefore posed a more serious risk of eventual disrup-
tion and fragmentation than de Gaulle did. But one
of de Gaulle's other accomplishments was to help
lay the foundation for a more flexible and pluralist order in the West, one which may be able to ac-
commodate and even thrive on the radical and often
innovative ideas offered by the Left in France and
elsewhere. This challenge has not materialized into a mature and irrefutable critique of the Western
order, but it may yet emerge as a crucial test for
national and international politics in the postwar period.

NOTES

1. A thorough discussion of the Socialist Party's evolution and structure since its swing to the extreme left in 1971 would unduly tax the reader's patience. See Vincent Wright and Howard Machin, "The French Socialist Party: Success and the Problems of Success," The Political Quarterly, Vol. 46, no. 1 (January-March, 1975), pp. 36-52; Jean-François Bizot's Au Parti des socialistes: Plongée libre dans les courants d'un grand parti, Paris: Bernard Grasset, 1975. The radical CERES minority obtained 25.4% of the votes at the Pau Congress in February 1975, and 24.21% at the Nantes Congress in June 1977.

2. This discussion naturally simplifies the diversity of views found in the PS, although the positions described here correspond to the attitudes and rhetoric of many party leaders. See the analysis by Richard Gombin, "Le Parti socialiste et la politique étrangère," Politique etrangere, no. 2 (1977), pp. 199-212.

3. See the Marchais report in Etienne Fajon, L'Union est un combat, Paris: Editions sociales, 1975.

4. For a concise Communist critique of the PS that reveals the PCF's own attitude, see Daniel Debatisse, "La Crise internationale, réalités et prétextes," Cahiers du Communisme, (December, 1977), pp. 32-43.

5. This kind of discussion was most prominent during Kissinger's administration of American foreign policy. See Charles Hernu's Soldat-Citoyen: Essai sur la défense et la sécurité, Paris: Flammarion, 1975.

6. It was surprising to see such notions discussed even by moderate Socialist Party military experts such as General Becam. See Becam's wide-ranging and confusing interview in Repères: Le Cahier du CERES (April, 1977), esp. p. 32.

7. Jean Marrane, L'Armée de la France démocratique, Paris: Editions sociales, 1977. This official defense policy statement of the PCF cites only Western threats to France.

8. Hernu, Soldat-Citoyen, passim.

9. See Robert Pontillon's "La Défense nationale française dans son environnement international: Contribution au débat sur la politique de défense," Comité directeur des 6, 7 novembre, 1976 (mimeo).

10. From the program of Mitterrand's Convention des institutions républicaines (CIR), entitled

Un Socialisme du possible, Paris: Seuil, 1970,
p. 96.
    11. Parti socialiste, Changer la vie: Pro-
gramme de gouvernement du Parti socialiste, Paris:
Flammarion, 1972, p. 198.
    12. Parti socialiste, Parti communiste, Mouve-
ment des Radicaux de gauche, Programme commun de
gouvernement, Paris: Flammarion, 1973, p. 85. For
a discussion emphasizing this more radical period
in Socialist Party foreign policy, see my article
"A Socialist Foreign Policy for France?" Orbis,
Vol. XIX, no. 4 (Winter, 1976), pp. 1471-1498.
    13. See Le Monde, November 11, 1977 for the
text of the motion finally approved in January
1978.
    14. Le Monde, January 10, 1978.
    15. The phrase is from Pontillon's report,
cited, p. 10.
    16. Charles Hernu, "Faut-il assurer la sécuri-
té de la France? Crises et menaces--perspectives
du Programme commun," Parti socialiste, Comité
directeur des 6 et 7 novembre, 1976, p. 14
(mimeo).
    17. See the Marchais report in Fajon, cited,
esp. pp. 95-96.
    18. See Jean Kanapa's report to the party Cen-
tral Committee, in Le Monde, June 24, 1976.
    19. In the forward to the program of his CIR,
Mitterrand noted that "the only possible path for
France is to combat the domination of the two blocs.
Everything that loosens their double grip is good
in itself." (Un Socialisme du possible, p. 21).
The PS program of 1972 takes up the same goal
(Changer la vie, p. 197.)
    20. Fajon, cited, pp. 96-97.
    21. See the Marchais interview in Le Monde,
March 3, 1978.
    22. See the Communist proposals in: Parti
communiste français, Programme commun de gouvernement actualisé, Paris: Editions sociales, 1978,
p. 143; also, Mitterrand's statement on the matter
in Le Monde, February 24, 1978.
    23. For the PCF view of these negotiations,
see: Pierre Juquin, Programme commun: L'Actuali-
sation à dossiers ouverts, Paris: Editions sociales, 1977.
    24. See the Pontillon report, "La Défense na-
tionale française," cited.
    25. For example, Jean-Pierre Chevènement, "La
Gauche, le gouvernement, le pouvoir," Le Monde,
July 17, 1976. CERES reservations about the

European Community are summarized in Annex I to
their motion presented at the party's 1977 Nantes
Congress and printed in Le Poing et la Rose, No. 62
(June, 1977), p. 25.

26. From Mitterrand's "Seven Options" of the
1965 presidential campaign, given in: Pascal Orly,
et.al., Les Chemins de l'unité, Paris: Tema-
éditions, 1974, p. 100.

27. Changer la vie, p. 206.

28. See Mitterrand's statements reported in
Le Monde on May 4 and 16, 1974.

29. Hernu, Soldat-Citoyen, p. 55.

30. See the Pontillon and Hernu reports, cited. Jean-Pierre Chevènement's contribution to this
meeting reflected the fact that the party's left-
wing elites were mostly in agreement. See: "La
Conception d'une défense indépendante dans la stra-
tégie du Programme commun," November, 1976 (mimeo).
Also interesting is the forthright discussion of
the party's new perspective by Gilles Martinet,
"Les Socialistes et la bombe," Le Nouvel Observateur, November 22, 1976.

31. The possibility was first raised in public
in remarks made by PCF defense expert Louis Bail-
lot, at a meeting of the Fondation pour les études
de défense générale in April 1976. See the initial
report in Le Monde on April 18-19, 1976 and quali-
fications in L'Humanité for April 19, as well as Le
Monde on April 20 and 23. Until the decisions of
May 1977, the most forthright Communist statements
in favor of the FNS came from Jean Elleinstein, the
party's leading "Eurocommunist." See Le Monde,
November 10, 1976.

32. See a summary of the Kanapa report and
Jacques Isnard's analysis in Le Monde, May 13,
1977.

33. For example, see the debate between
Jacques Huntzinger and Dominique Taddei in Faire:
Mensuel pour le socialisme et l'autogestion, nos.
21/22 (July-August, 1977), pp. 7-16. Also, Tad-
dei's article in Le Monde on January 7, 1978. Le
Nouvel Observateur (October 22, 1977) reported that
PS militants were hostile to nuclear power in all
its forms by a majority of 48% to 42%.

34. See, for example, the Marchais interview
in Le Monde on March 3, 1978, Marchais' statements
in L'Humanité on August 9, 1977, and Juquin, cited,
pp. 46-47.

35. The amendment submitted by this group was
defeated. It stated that "in the only foreseeable
hypothesis of a territorial intervention of the

USSR in Europe, Western solidarity is infinitely more of a deterrent than a specifically French threat." (Le Monde, January 8-9, 1978.)

36. The leadership's resolution was approved by 68.2% of the federation mandates voted at the convention.

37. From the defense motion text, in Le Monde, December 15, 1977.

38. See the Communist suggestions in Marrane, cited, and in Programme commun de gouvernement actualisé, cited.

39. Hernu's 1976 report, cited, also recommends construction of a sixth submarine. For the PS Defense Committee's brief recommendations, see L'Armée Nouvelle, September, 1974 (mimeo).

40. Le Monde, December 15, 1977.

41. Le Monde, January 10, 1978.

42. The Kanapa report also favors a sixth submarine and specifies that the Mirage-IVs should not be replaced as they wear out.

43. Le Monde, July 26, 1977.

44. These complicated problems are mentioned here only in passing. The interested reader should consult Geoffrey Kemp's Nuclear Forces for Medium Powers, parts I and II, London: International Institute for Strategic Studies, Adelphi Papers nos. 106 and 107, 1974.

45. Hernu, Soldat-Citoyen, p. 156.

46. Le Nouvel Observateur, August 18, 1977.

47. See comments by Marchais and Mitterrand in Le Monde, August 9, 10, and 12, 1977. The PCF also proposed abandoning the anti-city targeting strategy for the FNS, but quickly backed down under Socialist criticism. Communist proposals for a no-first-use of nuclear weapons commitment met a similar fate.

48. See the Marchais interview, Le Monde, March 3, 1978.

49. Général d'Armée G. Méry, "Une Armée pour quoi faire et comment?" Défense nationale, Vol. 32 (June, 1976), pp. 11-36.

50. See the president's speech to L'Institut des hautes études de défense nationale, printed in Défense nationale, Vol. 32 (July, 1976), pp. 5-20.

51. This was partially confirmed by government strategic guidelines (Le Monde, May 7, 1976), although officials have recently emphasized the trigger function of TNWs. (See remarks by Defense Minister Yvon Bourges before the National Assembly, in Le Monde, June 17, 1978.)

52. On the Pluton, see Hernu's 1976 report,

p. 6; also his <u>Chroniques d'attente</u>, cited.

53. Mitterrand stated, for example, "L'arme nucléaire, c'est la non-bataille." (<u>Le Monde</u>, January 10, 1978).

54. <u>Le Monde</u>, January 10, 1978.

3
The French Left and Europe

J. William Friend

Since the Union of the Left split in September 1977 and met defeat at the polls in March 1978, the term 'the Left' in France has had only a generic meaning; there is no longer a unified Left but rather two great parties, quarreling though committed to an ultimate resumption of collaboration. But the basis for the compromises that led to their alliance has been dissipated, and both the Communist Party (PCF) and Socialist Party (PS) think it more urgent to compete than to collaborate.

The European question is and has always been an issue dividing these two parties. Others in France see in it a choice for growth and political stability, weighed against a potential loss of sovereignty. For the Communists--and in part for the Socialists--the question of Europe implies much more: whether to accept Western Europe as a self-contained region, and concomitantly, whether to accept or combat the capitalism on which the European Community (EC) is based. Answers to these questions--always a function of domestic politics--have altered with time, from the original stand taken in 1957 on the Treaty of Rome to the need to work out and campaign on a Common Program of government. To be sure, the PCF remains deeply suspicious of the European Community and hostile to NATO, but given the waning of its loyalty to the Soviet Union it has nevertheless taken a new interest in Western Europe as a region. As to the Socialists, they have gone from the unquestioned support for the EC accorded by the old SFIO to a critical, often inconsistent, but basically positive view during the period 1971-1978. The result of uneasy and incomplete compromises among the constituent factions of the PS, Socialist policies may be further modified in the future by the ideological and power within the party. Finally, the election of a European parliament by universal suffrage in June 1979 has forced both the PS and the PCF into a renewed discussion of the meaning they intend to give to the concept of Europe.

THE PCF AND EUROPE: THE OLD, THE NEW, AND THE BORROWED

    We must begin with the Communist Party, for it has defined the terms of debate, first in the 1950s when the SFIO adhered to the Third Force against Gaullism and Communism, and after 1962 in a period of growing cooperation between Socialists and Communists that eventually paved the way to the alliance of 1972-1978. This latter period also saw the flowering of numerous political clubs, most of them further left than the SFIO, which merged later with the PS.[1]
    The European Economic Community was a child of the Cold War. The Treaty of Rome was signed on March 25, 1957, after the first thaw in the Cold War had led to upheaval in Poland and revolution in Hungary. The Soviet Union had no desire to see Western Europe strengthened, and a French Communist Party possessing no foreign policy ideas differing from Moscow's was automatically opposed to the Common Market. It had equally opposed its forerunner in the European Coal and Steel Community, finding both to be steps toward a supranational, integrated Europe under American domination. Any Europe not organized by international communism was by definition hostile to it, and must be combatted.
    These overriding considerations were joined to more detailed ideas developed by the PCF on the total perniciousness of the Common Market, expected to contribute to capitalist anarchy, monopoly, widespread unemployment, and loss of the social benefits enjoyed by French workers. In 1955, Secretary General Maurice Thorez had elaborated a theory that the Marxist law of relative and absolute pauperization of the working class was more valid than ever in France,[2] and PCF polemicists only saw in the Treaty of Rome a means for enforcing this process.
    By 1962, however, with the Common Market proving to be a success, the Italian Communist Party (PCI) began to reverse its earlier opposition to the Rome Treaty. "European integration," Luigi Longo told the PCI Central Committee in April 1962, "has been a fundamental factor in Italy's economic leap

49

forward"; and Giorgio Amendola to add that although "inevitably the EEC contributes to the process of capitalist concentration and centralization, causes crises of adjustment and sweeps away concerns which are working on excessively high unit costs ... all this necessitates, on the part of the working class, a European struggle."[3] The PCF, however, would have none of this yet, showing itself even more dogmatic than the Soviets, whose principal interest in opposing the Community was to keep Europe as weak and divided as possible. Holding to his pauperization theories, Thorez saw no benefits coming from the Common Market that did not go to monopolists, and taxed the PCI with revisionism for proposing "an allegedly positive policy calling for the 'insertion' of the working class and its organizations in the Common Market."[4]

During these years when the EC remained anathema to the PCF, the PCI developed a set of policies for the EC that fit into a larger European context. As Donald Blackmer has written, "for the Italian Communists, the Common Market represented essentially one of those institutions of the existing order with which, since they lacked the strength to destroy it, they had to come to terms. ... Italian Communist policy toward the EEC was also motivated by the conviction that European communism as a whole would grow increasingly ineffectual unless it managed to break out of national boundaries and to unite with other left-wing forces at an international level."[5] As it is known, the PCI has followed and developed this policy ever since.

The French Communists, in contrast, failed to devise a coherent strategy of their own toward Europe. In the earlier period, their policy was but a carbon copy of the Soviet one, with some French dogmatism added on to give it individuality if not independence. As time went on, of course, they were influenced by the PCI, and to some extent by the French Socialists--whose ideas were also influenced by those of the PCI. But the changes made in PCF European policies were grudging and inconsistent, producing the impression (in this as in other areas, then as now) that the party was being dragged forward by outside forces that it would have preferred to reject and escape.

Opposition to the EC did not mean total PCF rejection of its institutions. In 1963 PCF leader Waldeck Rochet demanded representation for his party in the European Assembly "so that we can bring to it our criticism, our propositions, to make heard the voice of the workers of France in the interest of peace and of all the peoples."[6] Such demand, however, represented a quintessentially Leninist view of the assembly as an institution useful only to exploit for propaganda reasons. In 1973, on the occasion of the entry of PCF deputies in the Assembly (where Italian Communists had gained representation four years earlier), PCF Politburo member Gustave Ansart made it plain to the Assembly that his party's hostility to the EC still prevailed: "The fifteen years of existence of the Common Market attest to a reality. Thirty-five multinational groups dominate economic life in Europe, and up to now the unification of the market and the simplification of the mechanisms of production have been made to the sole profit of the great multinational firms."[7]

Nevertheless, by the time Ansart spoke the PCF had revised its views on the Community, as a result of the negotiations on the Common Program signed in June 1972. Earlier that year, the negative vote urged by the PCF in the referendum on Europe called by President Pompidou, reflected the party's blanket opposition to the president's policies, an opposition shared by the PS which called for abstention. The results of the referendum, marked by a small turnout, encouraged both leftist parties to think that Pompidou was slipping.[8] Having thus made its point on domestic politics, the PCF was ready to trade compromises on Europe to achieve the Common Program it had long wanted.

The Common Program stated that a government of the Left would "participate in building the European Economic Community, its institutions and its common policies, with the will to act so as to free it from the domination of big capital, to democratize its institutions, to uphold the demands of the workers, and to orient Community achievements in the direction of their interests." The next sentence added, "the Left government will act to preserve, inside the Common Market, its liberty of action to realize its political, economic, and social program."[9] The nationalist flavor of the Common Program's language on Europe reflects the adaptation made by both parties of the Left to the ideas of their opponent Charles de Gaulle. It is often said, imprecisely, that there is no real debate in France over foreign policy, since everyone has become Gaullist. What has in fact happened is that the Left parties took over much of the form of Gaullist foreign

51

policy while selectively rejecting its content. De
Gaulle wanted an independent, capitalist France
which would play a leading role wherever possible.
Constituent parts of this policy fit Left politics
very well: coolness to the United States, rapprochement with the Soviet Union, pride in the continuing importance of France in European and Third
World affairs, and in general the high value placed
on national sovereignty. But the Gaullist policies
or attitudes were taken over by the Left not wholesale but piecemeal, as quilting materials which go
to make up a very different patchwork from that of
de Gaulle or his successors.

For the Communists, the resurgence of French
nationalism associated with de Gaulle led gradually
to a new emphasis which had earlier lain latent in
the French party. Nationalist feelings were never
absent from French Communism, though rejection of
noisy right-wing patriotism after World War I combined with internationalism to mask them; nationalism was sublimated in the proletarian internationalism that ended up as straight pro-Sovietism. The
Resistance experience, plus the discredit of the
right-wing patrioteers who in their vast majority
were pro-Vichy, opened the way for a change that was
slowed by the Cold War and the Stalin-cum-Thorez
cult.

"Mon parti m'a rendu les couleurs de la
France," wrote Aragon during the Resistance. This
phrase, with all its emotional overtones, was echoed
in the new slogan of the PCF that achieved increas-
ing currency in the late 1970s: "a party in the
colors of France." The PCF transition from proletarian internationalism to French nationalism was
both gradual and abrupt. It was gradual in the
sense that the party was newly susceptible to generalized nationalist feeling after World War II,
and after the Gaullist movement took away a million
of its voters, conscious at the top level of the
need to find some means to compete with the emotional appeal of Gaullism. After 1968, the PCF was also
increasingly doubtful of Soviet policy. But the
transition was also abrupt, because these problems
were largely suppressed in open discourse, so that
the "decision for Eurocommunism" the leadership
made sometime in the fall of 1975 looked like a
camp-meeting conversion. Once the decision was
made, however, the PCF plunged into the healing
stream of nationalism, seeking in it both a popular
and a theoretical replacement for the faded appeals
of internationalism. In May 1979, the theses for

the XXIII Congress made the party's independence an
integral part of its "international solidarity" with
the Soviet Union[10]--a far cry from the theses of
past years, even though it includes in practice support for most aspects of Soviet foreign policy.

The new identification with the nation-state
fits very well with the PCF's old aversion to any
European policies that could constrain it, when and
if it came to power, shared or total. Nationalism
now sputters in the language of the party's passionate opposition to enlargement of the powers of the
European Assembly: "the election would pull our
country into a process at the end of which an assembly composed of a majority of foreign deputies,
who are moreover reactionary, could dictate law to
and in the place of the French people and its
elected deputies."[11] And the warmup campaign for
the European elections of June 1979 that the PCF
began in the preceding winter was covered in
l'Humanité under such headlines as "Stop the Liquidation of France."

The compromise language on European questions
hammered out for the Common Program was not a major
influence in the European thinking of the PCF, although the need to sign the Common Program did provide an opportunity for the party to modernize its
antiquated approach to the EC and recognize it as a
reality. If the Union of the Left had stuck together, PCF policy on Europe would have been bent
by the constraints on practices and the policies of
the PS. As it was, the only concession made by the
PS on Europe after the signing of the Common Program was the decision not to fight parliamentary
approval of the law enabling direct elections to
the European Assembly--a concession largely vitiated
by the PCF's continuing opposition to those elections and enlarged powers for the Assembly.

Growing emulation of the PCI--a policy rejected in the 1960s--conditioned French Communist views
on Europe more than Socialist influence. In 1973,
PCF Secretary General Georges Marchais and his
Italian counterpart Enrico Berlinguer committed
their parties to "constructive participation" in the
EC, a phrase the Italians construed in a more ex-
tensive and positive sense than did the French.
The successes of the PCI in the divorce referendum
of 1974 and still more in the regional elections of
1975 did not go unnoticed in Paris; the PCF had
only to look across the Alps to find a model for a
successful, forward-looking Communist party--one
that dominated its socialist rival. The

long-standing icy relations between the two parties,
largely the fault of the French, now began to thaw.
In 1973-1974 there were seven high-level meetings
between them, but relations worsened again after
disagreements over the European Conference of Communist Parties, and even more sharply in early 1975
because of differing views on the situation in
Portugal.

November 1975 marked the PCF's great leap forward into Eurocommunism. Apparently despairing of
convincing its Soviet friends that revolutionary
solidarity was a two-way street,[11] the PCF faced a
difficult choice. The Soviets did not approve of
PCF tactics of all-out opposition to the Giscard
regime and alliance with the Socialists, but the
PCF leaders, after a season of wavering, had just
decided to press on with the alliance. A hard line
opposing both the Soviets and the frankly revisionist parties like the PCI and PCE might have been
logical, but from an electoral view was rather un-
promising. The PCF preferred to warm up relations
with the PCI. On November 15, 1975, Marchais flew
to Rome, where he signed a communique that in effect wrapped the cloak of Italian Communism around
the French party. Among other things, the PCF
promised to participate in initiatives which would
be "in favor of the democratization of the orienta-
tions and functioning of the European Economic Community, in favor of the progressive construction of
a democratic, peaceful and independent Europe."[12]

Despite its repeated subscription to similar
language, the PCF still looks at the Community with
grave doubts that anything can be made of such un-
promising beginnings. In July 1976, the PCF Politburo denounced the idea of electing a European
parliament by universal suffrage, repeating its
position thereafter at every opportunity. An article on the twentieth anniversary of the Treaty of
Rome in the authoritative PCF monthly Cahiers du
Communisme approvingly quoted l'Humanité's editorial
of twenty years earlier, which augured nothing but
disaster from the Common Market, ending with the
anniversary judgment "it is not exaggerated to think
that for the workers, peoples and nations concerned
the balance-sheet of the European Community is one
of bankruptcy."[13]

The PCF nevertheless intends to stay in the
European Assembly and fight "to work for the transformation of the European Communities in the interests of the workers." PCF deputies in the Assembly,
noted a PCF functionary, have neglected no chance

54

since 1973 to speak in favor of a Europe of social progress, liberty, and peaceful coexistence. But, he added gloomily, "It must be recognized that the Assembly has opposed a systematic and almost unanimous refusal to all these proposals."[14]

The implicit position of the Communist Party is that European institutions are a bad thing. But since they can be neither eliminated nor improved in current circumstances, they should be frozen until new conditions permit developments in a more favorable direction. Consequently, the PCF has vociferously opposed admission of Greece, Portugal, and especially Spain to the Community. The PCF conducted a noisily nationalist campaign ("poujadist," said the Socialists) against Spanish entry, warning--especially when campaigning in Southern France-- that farmers would be ruined by imports from countries with cheap labor. To questions of how this campaign fit together with communist solidarity, Marchais replied cooly that differences of opinion between communist parties were only natural, and that furthermore the Portuguese and Greek Communist Parties, as well as the Greek Socialist Party, were also opposed to their countries' entry into the Community.[15]

But the Italian tie still binds. In December 1978, the two parties came to an agreement on a joint platform for the European elections of June 1979. The text of their communique represents a victory of realism over propaganda, and may be a key document for the future. After noting persisting differences of opinion on the powers of the Community and its enlargement, the agreement reaffirmed the two parties' "common will to act together for great common objectives, which they will defend in future in the Assembly which emerges from the vote by universal suffrage."[16]

L'Humanité reported the agreement in the same issue that devoted a full page to Marchais' anti-EC barnstorming in Southern France under the headline, previously cited, "Stop the liquidation of France." Juxtaposition of the two articles sets the two poles of a policy which might easily be thought schizophrenic, but is instead merely irresponsible. In effect, an acknowledgment by the PCF that it must follow a course in the next European Assembly which is not just negatively Leninist, the program includes a specific list of measures to be enacted by the European parliament--some of them implying diminution of national sovereignty. Thus, the program calls for common Community legislation on

gradual reduction of the work week without lessened
pay (an idea advocated by many other European parties and unions), reduction of retirement age,
equalization of workers' benefits at the highest
Community level, equal rights and pay for men and
women. The two parties further call for a Community
statute proclaiming equal economic, social, political, and cultural rights for immigrant labor within
the Community, including residence rights, access
to employment, the chance for further technical education and promotion, schooling in the national
language,[17] and the extension of union and democratic rights including the right of free
association.

The communique calls for a new Community policy on agriculture, but gives no details. Past
meetings of the PCF and PCI on agriculture, and
multilateral conferences with other communist parties have usually produced generalized agreement on
modification of the Common Agricultural Policy, but
there appears to be little agreement on specifics.
The PCI is much more critical of the Common Agricultural Policy (CAP) than is the PCF, which is
equally mindful of those in western and central
France who have reasonably benefitted from it, as of
those in southern France who are hurt by current
policies. The main thrust of PCF agricultural policy is for higher prices paid to farmers, not for
the overall policy adjustment advocated by the
PCI.[18]

The agreement also proposes establishment of
public investigating committees of the European
parliament to control the activities of multinationals and banks--an American-style idea that might
appeal to many socialist parties. Finally, there is
the ritual call for support of detente and the Hel-
sinki agreement, controlled and balanced armament
reduction, the overcoming of the blocs, and friendly
cooperation with the Soviet bloc.[19]

In its emphasis on the rights of immigrant labor as in the stress on "the Assembly which emerges
from the vote by universal suffrage" the document
obviously owes more to the PCI than to the PCF.
But the idea of cooperating with the PCI in some
parliamentary struggles clearly has continued appeal for the PCF. How far that cooperation will extend is another question, and the PCI's appetite
for pragmatic compromise remains usually larger than
the PCF's. Thus, the pledge "to make the Europe of
the workers the result of the widest unity of Communists, Socialists, and democratic and progressive

workers' forces in the Community" is an Italian
formulation which means alliances with northern
Social Democrats, to say nothing of the French
Socialists.

Can any sense be made of the PCF view of Europe? Clearly, the party has no single and coherent policy. Instead, it has adopted some Italian
ideas even while it contradicts them with undimin-
ished nationalist rhetoric. Where, for example, the
PCI seeks good relations with all social democratic
parties, the PCF pursues its hopes of rebalancing
the French Left by accusing the PS of a swing to
the right and increased fealty to the European social democrats. The French Communists have sought
no friends among these parties and are unlikely to
find them.

If there is no consistent policy, there are
elements of several. The PCF sets a high value on
French sovereignty and French military isolation,
and seeks alliances with other communist parties in
Western Europe. The PCF has improved its relations
with the Italian, British, and Dutch parties, maintained the excellent ones it has always had with
the Belgians (who followed the French lead toward
an unsteady Eurocommunism), kept good relations
with the Portuguese and formally good but difficult
ones with the Spaniards, and forged new ties to
the Greek Communist Party. In Eastern Europe, the
PCF has good relations with the Romanians and particularly the Yugoslavs. As a result, the PCF follows not one foreign policy but parts of several:
for the EC with the Italians and Spaniards, but
against it with the British, Dutch, Portuguese, and
Greeks; for Eurocommunism with most of the communist parties in Western Europe, but against it with
the Greeks and Portuguese--and the East Germans and
Poles, who have increasingly replaced the Soviets
as regular interlocutors in the Eastern bloc.

Despite intermittently stormy relations with
the Soviets, who are restive under any criticism
from fraternal parties, the PCF regards Soviet foreign policy as a largely positive factor--from
which it follows that NATO serves only the mis-
chievous purposes of American or German imperialism.
A policy of systematic endorsement of Soviet positions has given way to one of substantial approval
of those positions. In this new phase the French
Communists may see in the Soviet connection, inter
alia, some of the advantages de Gaulle sought in
closer ties to the U.S.S.R. They want to keep the
balancing role of Soviet power in Europe against

American influence, though it is unclear whether
and at what point the PCF would oppose the Soviets
if the balance tilted toward Soviet hegemony in
Europe. The PCF certainly desires Soviet and East
European influence on the Federal Republic, seen by
the PCF sometimes as an agent of the U.S., sometimes
as an independent actor, and always as a menace on
the economic front. The PCF believes that the West
Germans will try to use the European parliament to
give the Federal Republic a hegemonic role in European affairs. They see in the German Social Democrats, and of course the Christian Democrats too,
archenemies of communism--forces which have already
intervened against communism in Spain and Portugal,
and would try to make of an enlarged Community a bul-
wark against communism all over Europe.[20]

There is thus something old, something new,
and much that is borrowed in the PCF's European policy. It faces so many different directions that it
is certain to evolve, even if there is no conscious
desire for innovation on the part of PCF leaders.
But how the contradictions will be resolved--
whether PCF policy will move closer to that of the
Italians, gravitate again toward the Soviets, or
form a hedgehog, bristling in all directions--still
remains impossible to predict.

THE THREE EUROPEAN LANGUAGES OF THE PS

If the European views of the communists were
influenced by the Soviets, de Gaulle, and the PCI,
they were little affected by those of the French
Socialists. Socialist policies, on the other hand,
were shaped first by the weight and then by the influence of the PCF. In the 1950s the SFIO sought
to build Europe as a stable, anticommunist bloc favorable to moderate socialism. The Treaty of Rome
was negotiated by the Socialist-led government of
Guy Mollet, and many leaders of the present Socialist Party remain loyal to this early commitment
even if, under the influence of Gaullist nationalism, they no longer advocate full European
integration.

The reformation of the SFIO initiated at the
Congress of Issy-les-Moulineaux immediately followed the disastrous presidential campaign of Gaston
Defferre in 1969. With Guy Mollet's tenacious grip
on the party's machinery at last broken, and with a
new secretary (Alain Savary) replacing him, most of
the leftist clubs and splinter groups which had

deserted the SFIO in the last years of the Fourth
Republic returned to the fold. Among the major
holdouts were the Convention des Institutions Re-
publicains (CIR), led by Francois Mitterrand, a
group usually allied with the SFIO but never a part
of it, and the Parti Socialiste Unifie (PSU), led
by Michel Rocard. At the 1971 Congress of Epinay,
Mitterrand brought in the CIR and, with the support
of the left-leaning CERES faction (Centre d'Etudes,
de Recherche et d'Education Socialistes), replaced
Savary as first secretary of a now renamed Parti
Socialiste. In 1974, Rocard joined the PS, carry-
ing with him a number of PSU militants but not his
party.

Thus, the new PS was created under the aegis
of electoral decline and gauchissement. Throughout
the sixties, the groups which had abandoned Mollet
had mapped out a new course for French socialism.
They found the social democracy of Northern Europe
neither ideologically nor practically desirable.
They rejected the Communist Party, but were heavily
influenced by communist ideas. Above all, they believed that gradualism was a bottomless swamp and
that a major break with capitalism was necessary.
The events of 1968 awakened many younger people to
radical politics, and in future years they flocked
to the PS. First in 1969, but increasingly after
1971, the new party was therefore dedicated to the
proposition that third force policies were politically and/or ideologically wrong, and that alliances
must instead be sought to the left.[21] Unlike Savary, Mitterrand made himself the effective advocate
of an agreement with the PCF, and a Common Program
of government was signed in 1972.

The new PS was forced to make numerous uneasy
compromises--not only with the PCF but also among
its own component factions. On Europe particularly,
the Socialists soon proved to be of several minds.
Already at Epinay, a heated debate focused on whether the PS should remain a member of the Socialist
International, and Mitterrand barely succeeded in
preserving party ties with an International deemed
to be hopelessly reformist and pro-Atlantic.[22] In
1972 at Suresnes, the PS debated whether France
should remain within the Atlantic Alliance or opt
for neutrality. There too Mitterrand prevailed--
but again by a small majority. In December 1973 at
Bagnolet, still another formal debate was needed to
define the party's European policy and achieve a
compromise on the ways in which true socialism could
be built in France even while maintaining the

country in a European community dedicated to
capitalism.

Thus, fundamental disagreement on Europe created what Jacques Huntzinger has called "the three
languages of French Socialism"--that of the old
SFIO, that of CERES, and a third used by Mitterrand,
which emerges, in Huntzinger's words, as "the gradual construction of an original foreign policy
through the interaction of extremely diverse positions through the influence of the first secretary."[23] Although in favor of a socialist Europe
organized along the lines of self-management,
CERES' language did not differ much from the PCF's,
and it readily dismissed Europe as the easy crea-
ture of capitalism, the multinational corporations,
and the United States. Mitterrand never adopted
the entire CERES vocabulary, but he did take over a
leftist, semi-Marxist one inveighed in particular
against the demons of multinational firms. To be
sure, the Communists did not take this leftist
language altogether seriously. They were pleased
to acknowledge it in 1972-1974, and, following a
break for quarrels, again in 1975-1977. But Mitterrand's strategy--on Europe as on other matters--
was all too obviously one of keeping everyone happy.
He alternated his emphasis between the CERES rhetoric on the one hand, and the pro-European SFIO
language on the other. Adopted by many PS leaders
who were especially anxious not to frighten moderate
voters, such language insisted that Europe must be
built first, and then made socialist. In fact, the
compromise on European policy adopted at Bagnolet
could be and was read as a combination of both tend-
encies--a commitment to go ahead with building
Europe even while proclaiming the principle of conditional participation in the Community.

After the defeat of March 1978, the pursuit of
the parallel course (still advocated strongly by
CERES and some others) continues to affect the party's attitudes toward Europe. Mitterrand believes
that the mixture of policies he has followed is the
only possible way to keep the party together and
prevent defection to the Communists. Others, however, now disagree and sharply criticize, in
Rocard's words, the "thought that the only thing to
do [is] to close ranks around certain basic certain-
ties, and that we [can] administer our 49.3 percent
of the vote while waiting for the next chance."[24]
As Rocard's ally Gilles Martinet put it, in an open
letter to Mitterrand:

The truth is that for a number of people you have only been repeating yourself, while Michel Rocard gave the impression of innovating. You, who are not a Marxist, are now paying attention to some singularly dogmatic ideas that recall Guy Mollet's kitchen Marxism. ... You, who are profoundly European, let some of your friends take initiatives that are too close to nationalist attitudes. You, who have always been so firm against crypto-communism, give the impression of relying on that wing of the party--the Joxe-Chevenement wing--which has always believed that it is in adopting positions as close as possible to the PC that one can compete with it.[25]

Joined by a number of figures in the party who come from diverse factional backgrounds, the Rocard-Mauroy group is not the SFIO redivivus. Its views on Europe were contained in a set of working documents presented to the PS executive bureau in late 1978.[26] According to these,

the problems facing the world from now to the end of the century are only linked in part to the capitalist mode of production. We are witnesses to the crisis of the model of development of the industrial society, whatever its specific forms of property. ... The rise of dangers in the military area can clearly not be attributed to capitalism alone ... Our will to break with capitalism must therefore not have an autarchic and isolationist meaning.

Thus, Rocard and Mauroy accept the context of the European Community, and condemn what they see as a wave of nationalism and chauvinism that is spreading all over France. Instead, they envision Europe as "a determinant framework for [the PS] strategy" since it is "in the first rank of [France's] environment." Such framework, it is argued further,

cannot be envisaged without the participation of the German Federal Republic. To reject this, explicitly or through ambiguous formulas like "no to a German Europe" or "no to a German-American Europe," can only reinforce the links existing between the Federal Republic and the U.S.A.

Accordingly, Rocard, Mauroy, and their allies

61

recommend a dialogue between the party and

the ensemble of northern European Social Democrats, who are the authentic representatives
of the labor world in their respective countries. Going beyond ideological discussions
where we do not see immediate solutions, it
seems possible to us to find points of agreement if we take up the concrete problems posed
by the crisis, in particular unemployment and
industrial evolution.

Yet, such dialogue with Northern Europe is to be
balanced by a further dialogue with Socialists and
Communists in Southern Europe--an obvious link with
the PCI strategy. "In sum," it is argued, the PS
"should stop presenting an analysis of the actual
social and political situation in Europe that is too
often static, and accept debate and dialogue without
fear of 'losing our souls.'" To suggest that capitalism is on its deathbed, it is written in a parallel document, is an illusion: breaking with capitalism is bound to be a complicated business....
"But it is characteristic that our party lets itself
be easily satisfied by simple speeches and declarations about these goals, without integrating them
sufficiently in a concrete program for governmental
action."
     This document was worth reviewing at length
because it marks the emergence of a new language, a
direct challenge to Mitterrand's intentional vague-
ness. In effect, it proved to be a declaration of
war against CERES, whose leader Jean-Pierre Chevenement promptly termed it "a rightwing offensive."[27]
Still close to the PCF on this issue, CERES calls
itself a partisan of a theoretical socialist Europe.
But the existing Europe of the EC is for CERES "an
autonomous relay for American domination, the instrument for regulation and modernization of world
capitalism."[28] Such relay passes by Bonn, and, predictably enough, CERES condemns any cooperation with
Social Democrats in the European parliament.
     Mitterrand's recent expression of his views on
Europe does not belie his reputation for artistic
fuzziness. In an interview with Le Monde, he con-
trasted the PCF's "categorical hostility" to Europe
with the policies of the PS which, he said, had a
clear position, did not quarrel with the Treaty of
Rome, and considered the Community a factor for
world peace. But, Mitterrand continued, the Community is above all a hunting preserve for big

capitalism. The Common Market has been beneficent on certain points, disappointing on others. "Inside this Europe that we accept, let us begin by defending French interests. It is better to use the instrument than to break it."[29] One is irresistibly reminded of Mr. Dooley glossing Teddy Roosevelt's views on the trusts: "The trusts, Hennessey, is monsters of hidjous mien, built up by th'enlightened enterprise of the men what has made our country great. On the one hand, I wud stamp thim under foot. On the other hand--not so fast."

The tactical element is of course prominent in all of the Socialists' intra-party declarations. Seeking a renewed alliance with Mitterrand, Chevenement found no problem with the party leader's positions, even if these appear to be closer to those of Rocard and Mauroy than to those of CERES. In truth, Chevenement's real worry is not over the future of Europe, as it is made clear in another phrase: "There is today an objective alliance between the neo-Stalinist tendency in the PCF and the neo-travailliste tendency in the PS, one that would lead, desired or not, to the reappearance of a Third Force."[30]

This takes us back to the Congress of Epinay and the policy of compromises Mitterrand used to build the PS. Fearing the unraveling of the party, Mitterrand is unwilling to renounce his old policies. On his left, the CERES, fearing slippage to the right if the PS does not stay on parallel course with the PCF, is a perennial candidate for closer embrace with Mitterrand. On his right, the Rocard-Mauroy group, in calling for innovative policies, had to defend itself against the accusation that it aimed at an eventual alliance with Giscard. The Metz Congress in April 1979 reconfirmed Mitterrand's leadership of the party, and opened the way for a renewed compact with the CERES. If the dynamics of compromise continue to operate, Mitterrand's policies on Europe are likely to remain, as they were before, pro-EC in general but full of contradictions in detail.

What can be said then of probable PS future policies on Europe, as an opposition party or potential member of the government? In the short run, the momentum of opposition will determine its attitude toward Giscard's European initiatives. For example, the PS position on the European Monetary System was largely a tactical-political one--a quick denunciation of Giscard's "failure" to negotiate a system which was more than a slightly modified

63

snake. In the present state of PS disunity, the
party could scarcely work out a position of its own
on so controversial an issue. Any attempt by Giscard to enlarge the powers of the European parliament (made improbable by Giscard's own problems
with the Gaullists) would also meet PS criticism--
again dictated by the logic of opposition.

Where PS initiative in the European parliament
is concerned, the party might seek an escape from
its factional problems in cooperation with the PCI--
something which might be at least minimally acceptable to the CERES and is specifically desired by
other factions of the party, as well as the Italian
Communists themselves. A joint communique on Europe
issued by the PCI and PCF suggests a number of possible agreements, either on specific issues or on a
programmatic basis. On many matters, the PS may
find it easier to work with the PCI than with the
PCF. The French Socialists would presumably make
the PCI more respectable to north Europeans, and
the PCI would make the PS more European.

The relations with the north Europeans already
exist, for Mitterrand worked hard to keep good relations with them, even while attempting to establish a southern bloc of socialist parties not opposed to alliances with communists. That particular
effort failed, because Spanish, Portuguese, Italian, and Greek Socialists did not have enough in
common with the French.[31] But the idea of a kind
of Eurosocialism which does not exclude cooperation
with communists retains considerable attraction for
the PS.

The PCI seeks such a bridge role, in which the
lineup of potential allies runs from the PCF on one
side of the spectrum, to the SPD on the other social democratic and integrationist European side.
This is evidently a highly unstable mixture. PCF
hostility to the PS may force the PS and even the
PCI to work more closely with the social democrats--
supposing that these parties want the alliance.

Because it is tied to a global compromise with
the PS, an agreement on Europe between the French
Socialists and the French Communists will be very
difficult--at least until the PCF is convinced at
last that internal quarreling in the PS and a wors-
ening in the economic situation of the country are
insufficient to restore the party to its previous
position of primacy on the left. In the meanwhile,
the European policies of the French Left remain
very much in flux, and those that can now be found
are tailored for the role of domestic opposition and

not for the responsibilities of government. All in
all, the PS continues to popularize the idea that
some kind of wider European commitment is a positive
step, while the Communists, though accepting the
institutions of Europe, campaign against a possible
future Europe as "an enslavement of France." Not
surprisingly, the discussions of 1978-1979 have left
the Left in France more divided on Europe than ever
before.

NOTES

   1. See Philippe Alexandre, Le Roman de la
Gauche (Paris, 1978) for an account of the Socialist-Communist rapprochement from 1962-1972.
   2. Philippe Robrieux, Maurice Thorez, vie
secrète et vie publique (Paris: Fayard, 1975),
p. 446.
   3. Cf. Simon Serfaty, "The Italian Communist
Party and Europe," Atlantic Community Quarterly,
Fall 1977, p. 278; R.E.M. Irving, "The European
Policy of the French and Italian Communists," International Affairs, July 1977, p. 414.
   4. Cf. Donald L.M. Blackmer, Unity and Diversity (Cambridge: M.I.T. Press, 1968), pp. 305-19
for a discussion of PCI evolution on the Market
question, and the details of PCF dogmatism.
   5. Ibid., pp. 326-27.
   6. Quoted in "Les Communistes français et
l'Europe," Bulletin des Communistes Français à
l'Assemblée des Communautés Européennes, No. 1,
p. 1.
   7. Ibid.
   8. Jean Poperen, L'Unité de la Gauche, 1965-
73 (Paris: Fayard, 1975), pp. 379-84.
   9. Programme Commun de Gouvernement (Paris:
Editions sociales, 1972), p. 177.
   10. Supplement to L'Humanite, February 13,
1979, p. VIII.
   11. Gérard Streif, "Marche Commun--du Traite
de Rome au Projêt d'Élection de l'Assemblée Européenne,"Cahiers du Communisme, April 1977, p. 71.
   12. See the article by Jean Kanapa outlining
this logic, "Les Communistes Français et l'Interna-
tionalisme Prolétaire," France Nouvelle, March 29,
1976.
   13. Streif, op. cit. Gérard Streif is a staff-
er for the Foreign Policy section of the PCF Central
Committee apparat, concerned with European affairs.
   14. Ibid.

15. L'Humanité, November 18, 1978. Marchais made a number of speeches on this topic.

16. Ibid.

17. The phrase is ambiguous, but almost certainly means the native language of the worker.

18. Cf. Jean Flavien, "Un exemple à méditer," France Nouvelle, February 28, 1977, pp. 12-14; Ibid., July 24, 1977, comments on a question by Paul Lespagnol, p. 18. Both men are collaborators of the Central Committee apparat's Central Agriculture Section. Also see communiques of the Ferrara meeting of Western CP's on the Common Agricultural Policy, October 11-12, 1976, and the PCI-PCF meeting on agriculture in Paris, June 6, 1977, both cited in Les Communistes français et l'Europe, No. 1. Also Giuseppe Vitale, "Politica agricola CEE: non bastano ritocchi occorre una svolta," Rinascita, March 18, 1977, pp. 13-14.

19. L'Humanité, December 18, 1978, and L'Unità, same day.

20. Cf. Catherine Mills, "Ambitions et moyens de l'impérialisme allemand," Cahiers du Communisme, January 1977, p. 98.

21. Poperen, op. cit., p. 323.

22. Jacques Huntzinger, "The French Socialist Party and Western Relations," in Werner Feld (ed.), The Foreign Policies of West European Socialist Parties (New York: Praeger, 1978), p. 68.

23. Ibid., p. 73.

24. Le Monde, February 10, 1979.

25. Ibid.

26. Ibid., December 23, 1978.

27. Ibid., January 4, 1979.

28. Ibid., December 19, 1978. Jacques Sandeau and Pierre-Luc Seguillon, "Les Socialistes dans l'Opposition à Strasbourg?".

29. Ibid., January 6, 1979.

30. Ibid., January 4, 1979.

31. Huntzinger, op. cit., p. 75.

4
The French Left
and the Third World

Ronald Teirsky

Though of limited political relevance after
the legislative elections of March 1978, an examination of Socialist and Communist rhetoric on
France's relations with the Third World continues
to be useful insofar as the two opposition parties
themselves are concerned.* This essay is therefore
concerned with such questions as: In what ways did
PS and PCF Third World policies agree or disagree
during the "Union of the Left," 1972-1977? On balance, did the interparty negotiation of Third
World policy reflect general agreement or disagreement? After these questions have been answered, it
will be possible to proceed with an analysis of the
uses or functions of Third World policy for the two
parties, taken separately and in their alliance of
frères enemis What does the elaboration of Third
World policy tell us about the general nature of
the two parties and their disagreements? Has the
Socialist Party chosen to appear relatively moderate or relatively radical in its Third World policy? Has its rhetoric been generally doctrinal or
generally technocratic? That is, has the PS Third
World policy been more an authentication of radical
credentials and part of the ideological struggle
with the Communists, or has it been concerned
greatly with economic calculations of means/ends
relations, designed to reassure domestic and foreign Establishments that the PS would act responsi-
bly in government? On the Communist side, has the
PCF chosen to appear more Soviet-aligned or more

*Acknowledgment: I would like to thank Mr. Richard
Goldberg, a graduate student at the University of
Massachusetts, Amherst, who did much of the re-
search for this article.

"Eurocommunist" in its Third World policy? To what
extent does PCF Third World policy begin with, or
reject out of hand the established "Western" or
"capitalist" institutions of which France is a
member?

In sum, given the general priority of domestic
over foreign policy in French electoral politics,
and given the secondary status of Third World demands for redistribution in the foreign policies of
industrialized states generally, what were the PS
and PCF trying to gain, or to prove, in their programmatic discourse on the Third World?

THIRD WORLD POLICY IN THE "COMMON PROGRAM"

It is common knowledge that the French Socialist and Communist Parties--their Union of the
Left alliance and Common Program notwithstand-
ing--have espoused fundamentally different conceptions of a socialist order. The difference between the basically "vanguardist" Communist politics and the Socialist Party's liberal core leaves
us hardly surprised to find certain disagreements
as well on matters relating to the developing
world, whatever mutual policies and viewpoints issue from the common socialist intention. Yet in
the impasse of June-September 1977, when negotiations to update the Common Program ended in a sud-
den self-liquidation of the five-year-old alliance
(except for a last minute agreement on reciprocal
withdrawals of candidates in the second ballot),
Third World policies were not much at issue. One
can say, then, that either the Common Program, so
far as it went, indeed laid out certain genuinely
shared perspectives, or Third World policy never
became seriously contentious because its significance was recognized to be basically symbolic, the
price of agreement being both inexpensive and pay-
able in some undetermined future (if at all), and
the benefits of agreement (however modest) still
worth having.

The Common Program asserted that the PS and
PCF were mutually interested in a major restructuring of relationships between France and the developing areas.[1] The Program called for a radical new
policy of cooperation based on genuine independence
and noninterference in internal affairs. It urged
an end to colonial and neocolonial domination, and
in particular recognized that France faces special
responsibilities in its former colonial realm,

68

first of all in Africa. The two parties promised
a policy favoring public aid and development over
the private sector, directing the benefits towards
the genuine needs of the recipient states rather
than the narrow requirements of French commercial
interests. It also called for a revision of the
associated status arrangements negotiated between
EEC states and the developing countries, the so-
called Yaoundé II agreements.[2]

Nothing was said about national liberation
movements, other than a brief reference of support
for independence struggles. Nor was there any reference to France's dependency on the Third World
for raw materials, reflecting the fact that the
document was drafted prior to the quadrupling of
oil prices by the OPEC governments. In sum, the
Common Program contained but a few pages of gener-
alities on Third World policy: more concrete perspectives must therefore be sought elsewhere.

That the Common Program relegated Third World
issues to its back pages should not mislead us into
thinking that such issues are peripheral to French
parties and political life. It was, after all, decolonization and the evolution of new relationships
with Indochina and the African states which so
traumatized French political life during the Fourth
and early Fifth Republics. Throughout this era of
decolonization, the PCF remained supportive of the
general line taken by the world communist movement
towards the Third World: entirely sympathetic to
the major national liberation confrontations of the
period, and supportive of Marxist or socialist
movements over others, except where the Soviet government for whatever reason established a different
line. The party mobilized with an effectiveness
naturally limited by its permanent opposition
status: street demonstrations, pronouncements,
action in parliament, or participation in far-flung
world conferences.

Yet, in spite of these and other such initiatives as the party's refusal to load ships bound
for Indochina, the credentials of the PCF on issues
of colonialism suffered from numerous equivocations.
Certainly, classical doctrine was not always of
help in sorting out the issues. Early Marxism
barely dealt with the subject of national liberation. Only late in life did Marx concern himself
with the national independence problems of India
and Ireland. Lenin had wanted to bring the revolution to the colonies, but was unsure whether colonial liberation was a one-stage or two-stage

69

operation: Would they move to socialism directly, or did they have to develop a national bourgeoisie? Stalin himself displayed much suspicion toward such independence leaders as Ghandi. He saw them as vassals of capitalism, leading independent nations, but still dependent on their ex-colonial rulers. Only under Khrushchev were the new nonaligned states accepted as basically compatible with the interests of the Soviet bloc.

It should not be surprising, then, that for decades a mode of revolutionary paternalism prevailed in the French Communist attitude toward less developed lands. If socialism was to come to the colonial realms, it would arrive derivatively, through the French people themselves achieving socialism. The empire would be socialized rather than decolonized.

Furthermore, this conception had the approval of the USSR, whether for reasons of doctrine or raison d'état. One need only cite the de Gaulle-Molotov meeting of May 1942, at which the Soviet Union pledged itself to a future framework where all the peoples of the French colonies would yield to de Gaulle's leadership.[3] Early PCF policy conformed to this scheme, calling for the retention of colonies within the French Union, although paying lip service to a degree of autonomy. Even Algeria was not recognized as a national entity by the Communists.

At the Xth PCF Congress in 1945 following the Liberation, party leader Maurice Thorez called for a "union in freedom, trust and brotherhood between the colonial peoples and the people of France." While holding out some vague idea of self-determination, he basically espoused Lenin's dictum, set in a different time and place, that "the right of divorce did not mean the obligation to divorce." During the early stages of the Indochina war in 1946-1947, Thorez, then a vice president in the Tripartite Council of Ministers, and the other Communist ministers supported military credits for the war on the insurgents.[4]

In the years following World War II, the SFIO likewise underwent agonizing contortions in adjusting to France's declining influence. But unlike the PCF which remained in permanent opposition after May 1947, the SFIO was broadly implicated in the Indochina war, and it was a Socialist prime minister, Guy Mollet, who led France into the 1956 Suez imbroglio. (Anti-colonialist critics within the SFIO had been defeated at a party congress that year.[5]) Indeed, Mollet went on to be a major supporter of the war in Algeria, despite his earlier repudiation of the Algérie française slogan. François Mitterrand too, as minister of the interior, could not avoid being tainted by the Algerian war, as he declared from the National Assembly rostrum in 1956: "La seule négociation possible, c'est la guerre!"[6]

Such actions taken by the SFIO during the difficult years of the Fourth Republic contradicted a socialist rhetoric of solidarity and hardly enhanced its credibility as a friend of the Third World. Accordingly, the new PS fundamentally updated its conceptions of the Third World's relationship to the developed states generally (as will be shown later)[7] and to France specifically. In this case, a separate program was set forth in 1972, a program highly critical of policies which favored French business interests over the requirements of the underdeveloped states, and remained subordinated to US policy wishes. Before examining the key elements of the PS program, it might be useful to turn first to the PCF's own analysis of Third World issues.[8]

THE COMMUNISTS AND THE THIRD WORLD

According to the Communists, French capitalism emerged from World War II in a condition of dependency, stagnation, indebtedness, and general political impotence. To regain their position, the monopolies needed a larger base for their activities.[9] Gaullism was the political force that was able to accomplish this objective, chiefly by utilizing the Treaty of Rome and the new relationships deriving from it. As the PCF describes it, the new Fifth Republic went on to establish firm positions: strengthening the currency, reducing debt, building a nuclear force, disengaging from the integrated NATO command, and encouraging advanced sectors of technology.

Gaullism required a Third World policy to meet new realities; hence it began to inaugurate agreements of cooperation and aid. The PCF argues that de Gaulle was actually setting forth relations of a neocolonial character with the newly independent states. The goal was first, to keep them within a capitalist mode of development; second, to extend French economic penetrations; and third, to overcome France's backwardness in relation to its

rivals.[10]   At its disposal, France had a number of
assets: a forum in the Security Council of the UN;
the world's third-ranking nuclear arsenal (the only
European power with diverse atomic forces, both
strategic and tactical); neocolonial positions and
a network of bases permitting the deployment of
forces in Africa, the Caribbean, and the Indian
Ocean.
     In Africa, the Mid-East, and Indian Ocean,
France pursued its penetrations through a policy of
"cooperation," according to such Communist analysis.
The young states of the Third World were seen as
"privileged zones" for commercial activity.   Special targets were those states considered politically secure.   Thus, French capital was directed
toward the Ivory Coast, Gabon and the Zaire of
Mobutu, or South Africa, Iran, Egypt--and even as
far away as Indonesia and Brazil.   Raw materials
were a prime target.   But French imperialism was
"equally interested in the presence of an enormous
workforce at its disposal, of which the conditions
for exploitation are considered especially
advantageous."[11]
     Despite its limited success, imperialism (both
French and that of its rivals) continues to confront the inexorable opposition of national liberation movements.   The PCF is unswerving in its ideological support of anticapitalist sovereignty, and
the right of Third World nations to control their
own resources and build their national economies.[12]
In this struggle the developed states seek to destroy the unity of the young nations whose coales-
cence derives from the demands they are making on
the developed Western nations at the various North-
South confrontations.   In particular, the imperialist countries manipulate the reactionary regimes of
the Third World against progressive ones (i.e.,
those with a socialist orientation).[13]   Witness
Zaire or South Africa summoned to defend a particular faction in Angola, or Hassan's Morocco employed
to preserve the status quo in Zaire.
     The Communists have also rejected emphatically
the West's economic strategy toward the OPEC cartel.
When OPEC raised oil prices, the West countered
with price increases on industrial products.   As a
result, the non-oil producing states ran up an ex-
traordinary indebtedness to the industrial nations.
From the PCF perspective, the situation stems from
a deliberate Western strategy designed to heighten
the dependency of the poorer countries.   In con-
trasting French Communist analysis with that of the

Socialist Party, one is struck by the persistence
with which the former discern deliberate strategies
and conspiratorial forces at work in undermining
Third World welfare. Thus, although equally concerned about the debt problem, the Socialists would
hardly go so far as to attribute these imbalances
to a deliberate ploy of conspiratorial forces. Instead, they blame the pervasive influence of market
forces, and find in such alarming debt level the
reflection of an inherent malfunctioning of the
world capitalist economy as it was originally
structured under the Bretton-Woods framework.

In general, the Communists now see some ground
for optimism. Not only was the MPLA success in
Angola a key victory for a national liberation
movement, but PCF analysis took note of the fact
that the US for domestic reasons (including frus-
trations over Watergate and the Vietnam defeat) was
powerless to change the outcome. In other words,
they conclude that 'imperialism's means of direct
intervention' have been diminished.[14] Furthermore,
they saw that the political weight of the socialist bloc countries--in the form of international
solidarity (and here they are referring to the capacity of, for example, the Soviet Union and Cuba
to provide aid to Third World liberation movements)--must be taken into greater account.[15]

"Imperialist Rivalry"

While it is only natural that the Communists
applaud any French withdrawal from an area of former interest (for example, France has withdrawn from
certain Indian Ocean outposts in recent years),
there is one important caveat: that some other rival imperialist power might well step into the vac-
uum. It is hardly a victory for the forces of
world socialism if France makes a withdrawal, only
to have the United States, the Federal Republic of
Germany, or Japan supplant the former role of
France. Madagascar, for instance, received its independence in 1960. Yet between that year and
1972, trade (measured in both imports and exports)
increased over threefold with the dollar zone.[16]
Any evidence of West German penetration into former
French realms in Africa is a particular irritant
to the PCF. Communist analysts make a strong case
that the US has stepped into too many former French
(and British) realms in the Indian Ocean. Soviet
gains are generally ignored, or are endorsed as
gains for "world socialism" and the alliance of
socialism and national liberation.

73

The PCF is a highly vocal opposition party,
and any sally by the Giscard d'Estaing leadership
into the Third World is generally treated with
scorn. For example, the PCF was highly critical of
Giscard's threat in May 1975, to land three regiments in Lebanon within forty-eight hours if the
need arose. In fact, the PCF tends to oppose any
attempt by Giscard to assert France's role in world
crises. At the same time, and inconsistently, they
ridicule any signs of impotence by the regime.
When the government does assert a role in the Third
World, such as airlifting Moroccan troops to Zaire
in April 1977, it is generally condemned as an
American-inspired adventure. At other moments, it
is argued that Giscard treats Africa as a special
preserve, a source of raw materials vital to the
development of Western industry. When he under-
takes a military move on the continent, he is
therefore seeking to maintain compliant regimes in
order to assure access to these sources.

The Indian Ocean Region

Up to the disintegration of the European em-
pires, the Indian Ocean region was a traditional
area of Anglo-French influence. Yet, despite her
withdrawal, France retains a residual influence
which concerns the PCF all the more vividly as the
party holds a leverage of its own through contacts
in the region with local communist parties.
The French naval and military presence in the
Indian Ocean is quite modest compared to US and
Soviet activity. Nevertheless, French policy mak-
ers continue to regard France as a power with an
international role to play. Even in an era of
superpowers she seeks a voice in world affairs, rejecting what former Foreign Minister Michel Jobert
used to call "the condominium of the superpowers."
In keeping with such notions, France's outposts in
the Indian Ocean lie along the sea lanes from the
Suez Canal and the Cape route around Africa. Her
chief oil supplies stem from the Perisan Gulf, and
they require some means of protection, should the
need arise. Then, too, as a nuclear power France
has conducted atomic tests in the region, requir-
ing monitoring stations in that ocean. As a naval
power, French ships will from time to time establish their presence through a politique du pavil-
lon, designed to impress those who once had ties to
France or who continue to speak the language.
France granted independence to Madagascar in

1960, but was able to insist on retaining certain economic, military, and cultural arrangements. Up until 1975, France even retained its large air and naval facility at Diego Suarez as well as the inland base at Tananarive. Since 1975, at which time Madagascar insisted on full neutrality, the Navy has been shifted to a new base at St. Denis on the Island of Réunion, which has remained a Department of France. Its harbor, however, is considerably inferior.

While France was also compelled to yield bases on the Comoro Islands, it retains a base on Mayotte, which is on the northern entrance to the Mozambique Channel (opposite Madagascar). In any conflict, the area would be quite strategic, since it dominates the sea lanes along the eastern coast of Africa. Its significance was not overlooked by L'Humanité, which noted that (as of 1976) a million tons of oil flow through the channel daily, destined for Europe and the US.[17] Currently, there is a battalion at Mayotte, and the base is considered easily reinforceable. France has also allocated considerable sums to equip militarily some of the smaller islands in the Indian Ocean, such as Glorieuse, Tromelia, Europa, and others off Madagascar.[18]

Djibouti, on the Gulf of Aden, at the vital mouth of the Red Sea, is a further strategic site that has not escaped the attention of the Communists. In June 1977, this area of the Horn of Africa received its independence after seventy-one years of French rule. The event was, of course, pleasing to L'Humanité, but the press account went on to note that "many booby traps" remain in the arrangements.[19] The journal charged the Giscard government with imposing an improper division of the territory and seeking to manipulate the government structure. Most importantly, the Communists are keenly suspicious of Giscard's intent to retain the French base there. They point out that the force stationed in Djibouti is essentially operational. Moreover, Djibouti has an excellent military harbor, and its garrison is considered quite reinforceable by a force d'intervention. Giscard's pledge to guarantee the security of the new state was viewed by the PCF as a threat to nearby socialist-leaning Somalia.[20] The Communists argue that both the US and France will seek to weaken any socialist-oriented regime installed in that area of the Horn. They also suggest that the adamantly antisocialist regime of Saudi Arabia, strengthened

75

with Western arms, would willingly play the role of protector for the new state of Djibouti.

In terms of overall Indian Ocean policy, the PCF appears convinced that France is determined to maintain what influence it can. By maintaining a permanent military presence capable of intervening directly in crisis situations, the PCF argues that France is actually opposing the right of new nations to settle freely their own affairs. At the same time, France is able to maintain its dominion over raw material resources and supply routes, chiefly for petroleum.[21]

The Communists reply that they would be able to offer a "more democratic policy in the Indian Ocean, a region where France could make a positive contribution towards peace and security." In the analysis cited above, the author, Michel Carlot, goes on to note that the problem of assuring peace in that area has already been posed at the United Nations. Here, he is probably referring to the "Zones of Peace" Resolution of December 23, 1973, which sought to define the military presence of the great powers in the Indian Ocean. It should be noted that the United States, Soviet Union, France, and Britain all abstained on this resolution, and that great power negotiations in 1978 have broken down, both reflecting and stimulating the current instability in the area.

In taking note of US activity in the Indian Ocean region, the Communists have expressed criticism of the NASA base for satellite tracking at Madagascar, as well as other US naval dispositions in the ocean.[22] This sensitivity is, of course, an echo of Soviet apprehensions.[23]

Africa, Energy, and the PCF

Not surprisingly, the Communists have continued to observe critically French political and diplomatic activity in the Arab world, where France's energy needs have in recent years made that region the source of 85 percent of her petroleum. The PCF has suggested that the Giscard regime has pursued a strategy of opposing non-oil producing states (the so-called "Fourth World") to the producing states. Thus, Giscard has led the poorer, nonproducing nations to believe that their large payments deficits stem from oil price increases made by the producing countries. In reality, the PCF holds, 65 percent of these Fourth World deficits (in 1975) stem from their trade imbalances with the OECD nations.

76

The French government is further charged with favoritism towards certain oil-producing states. It is the Arab states of the Gulf and Iran which are favored over the more nationalized (and more socialist-oriented) regimes of Algeria, Iraq, and Libya.[24]

It can reasonably be anticipated that a Communist energy policy for France (one which would probably be compatible with their Socialist partners) would seek to increase the proportion of petroleum supplied to France by Algeria and Iraq. But in spite of the evident distaste the Communists have for other Arab states, it does not seem likely that they would be in a position to foreclose entirely those areas as continuing suppliers of France. The Soviet Union itself continued to receive oil deliveries from Iran, despite its opposition to the Shah's regime.

The PCF in general still calls for vastly expanded trade arrangements with the Soviet Union and other Eastern bloc states. However, it has not been suggested that the Soviet Union could itself become a supplier of petroleum to France. Such a prospect is unlikely, since the USSR has already overextended itself as a supplier of energy to Eastern Europe.[25]

In sum, any left-wing energy policy seems highly unlikely to escape France's fundamental dependence on Arab oil. Any left-wing government party would be compelled to accept such working relations, if not more, with the states of that region. The PS may soon be faced with these problems as a practical matter; its judgments have been both complex and tortured. The PCF, on the other hand, continues to speak as a party of permanent opposition. When France furnishes technical aid or weapons to Saudi Arabia and encourages French development projects in the Arab Emirates, such as Qatar, the PCF proclaims that Giscard is simply fulfilling his role of establishing France's status in the international capitalist-imperialist order and protecting French multinationals.

Algerian Relations

While aspects of earlier Communist and Socialist Party policies towards Algeria have already been touched upon, the problem requires further examination. Both parties feel (and often express) a special affinity with that part of North Africa for historical, geographical, and (in the case of the PCF, especially) ideological reasons.

77

Nationalizations. The Boumédienne regime, less friendly with Giscard than with either de Gaulle or Pompidou, was considered by the Communists to have waged a legitimate independence struggle for control of its national wealth and resources. Historically, the Communists argued early on that the Evian accords served a French intention to retain France's control of Algerian national wealth. Hence, the PCF applauded such decisive steps as Algeria's nationalization of the foreign oil and gas facilities of ELF-ERAP and Compagnie Française des Pétroles in 1970-1971.[26] Algeria, in effect, implemented policies in 1971 that Mossadegh had been powerless to do in 1951-1953 in Iran, reaffirming the Communist argument that the world relation of forces is not what it was in 1951. In terms of Third World symbolism, these nationalizations demolished the myth of invulnerable monopolies: developing countries could, indeed, exploit their own wealth. Furthermore, such steps served to push Syria and Iraq to move in a similar direction.

These, then, were the major positive trends noted by the Communists in the realization of the Algerian revolution under Boumédienne. However, Algeria's recent signing of several protocols with the United States, West German, and Japanese multinationals has caused concern among the Communists, who are quick to blame France's waning trade ties. They point out that after Algeria nationalized its oil industry, France considerably lowered its purchases of petroleum, shifting its supply sources to Saudi Arabia and the Gulf. As noted, the PCF would want to redirect French trading patterns towards socialist-oriented Third World countries-- at least to the extent that they could. The huge and long-term Algerian offer, made at the end of 1978, to supply natural gas to the United States could only increase PCF doubts about the future of a "socialist" Algerian policy, doubts made more concrete with Boumédienne's death on December 27. The PCF thus may be led to revise its position on Algeria and on oil supply generally.

PCF-FLN Ties. One of the more practical, if still highly Byzantine aspects of the PCF's involvement with the Third World is the network of proto-state relations enjoyed by the party and its leading functionaries with an assortment of heads-of-state, political parties, and liberation movements around the globe. In 1972-1977, the PCF acted as a potential government party, standing ready in the wings, and carefully guarding the special links between itself and the FLN. These ties, which had been somewhat strained following 1965, improved considerably during those years. In 1972, for example, PCF Politbureau member Raymond Guyot led a delegation to the FLN. Among other things, he reiterated what a new energy policy would be under the program of an "advanced democracy" in France: namely, that the public sector in France would assume majority financial participation in ERAP and CFP, and that henceforth, agreements would be freely negotiated without any hint of neocolonialism.

Two years later, Boumédienne invited Georges Marchais and Jacques Denis to Algiers for wide-ranging talks.[27] According to journalists' accounts, the discussions had almost the flavor of a government-to-government parley (not entirely surprising given the near-victory in the French presidential elections that year of the Socialist François Mitterrand, and the strong government aspirations of the PS-PCF alliance).[28] Among other things, Marchais noted that the Algerian nationalizations had led to a series of French retaliations regarding emigration policy and Algerian wine exports. He made it clear that such "neocolonialist" pressures would not be applied by a left-wing government. Instead, he proposed an era of specific contract commitments to purchase Algerian products, based on long-term loans at low interest rates, without political conditions attached. In April 1977, the CGT (labor union) Secretary General Georges Seguy made a similar trip to Algiers to discuss problems of racism against Algerian workers in France, as well as topics earlier raised during the Marchais talks.[29]

When PCF delegations have met with their Algerian counterparts, it has been not merely to raise issues of interest to their hosts, nor to issue resounding pronouncements on the urgency of Third World liberation. Instead, there has often occurred important quid pro quo, with the Algerian side affirming positions more crucial to the French Communists. The PCF, after all, as a nonruling European party is excluded from various world forums. By lining up governmental support from a friendly Third World state, it seeks to increase both its prestige and its leverage as a political force, domestically and internationally.

Africa

We have seen that the PCF often flaunts its not entirely unambiguous credentials as a historical foe of colonialism around the globe. It plays heavily the chord of its struggle against France's war in Morocco in the 1920s and its opposition to the wars in Indochina, Algeria, and Suez. In the 1970s, Africa has continued to be an important arena of anticolonial activity. We have already touched on certain portions of African policy while discussing the cases of the Indian Ocean and Algeria, but a closer look is now in order.

Standard Communist positions include:

- Opposition to the French government collusion with Portuguese forces in furnishing aid to South Africa.
- Condemnation of French military intervention in Chad and the sending of paratroops to Gabon.
- Opposition to Biafra's secession from Nigeria.
- Criticism of Pompidou for expanding French investments in Africa under the cover of aid and cooperation agreements.
- Revision of accords reached between France and African states, if they were imposed in negotiations that were essentially unequal because these states had recently achieved independent status.

In terms of cultural relations with former French areas, the PCF remains quite suspicious of the official policy of francophonie, arguing that it masquerades neocolonialist objectives and in the long run only perpetuates dependency. At times, the Communists will allow that they would encourage the teaching of French, but only as a secondary language. A "democratic" France, they maintain, would attempt to promote the rebirth of indigenous national cultures. On this issue they are in essential agreement with the PS.

Zaire and the Issue of National Liberation. Clearly, a major area of PCF-PS disagreement on Third World conceptions has been over movements of national liberation. Reactions to crises in several African states in the mid-1970s can serve as an illustration of these different perceptions. Thus, the Communists have made much of the fact that the

PS (like most West European social democracies) generally supported the FNLA forces and UNITA against the MPLA in the struggle for control in Mozambique upon Portuguese withdrawal. In the spring of 1977, the same discordance surfaced when Giscard helped out the Mobutu regime in Zaire. From the beginning, the PCF alleged French collusion with Belgium, and asserted that Giscard had attempted to solicit American intervention. When it was finally disclosed that French transports had been made available to King Hassan II to fly 800 Moroccan troops from Kinshasa to Shaba Province in Zaire, the PCF's reaction was violent. Giscard was charged with deceiving the French people, violating international law, and acting without parliamentary authority. Robert Ballanger, leader of the PCF National Assembly group, demanded that the president appear before that forum.[30] The Socialists also opposed the venture, but there were differences of tone and substance. National Secretary Claude Estier would only go so far as to note that there had been no consultation with parliament, that Giscard had presented a fait accompli. Other PS leaders, such as Jean-Pierre Cot, said that Giscard was attempting to become Africa's policeman. Regarding the Soviet role in Africa, there are also important differences between the two parties. The PCF freely justifies Soviet (and Cuban) efforts, while the Socialists (a majority of them, in any case) remain less than satisfied with these penetrations, reflecting their somewhat agonized but nonetheless quite clear commitment to Western interests in the overall world balance.

Latin America

The Communists, for obvious reasons, do not regard Latin America as a priority area for French neocolonialism. Yet they are concerned, and are quick to note, that of all the historical European colonizers in that area, France remains virtually the only one with a toehold.

Politically, French influence is vestigial, manifested in retention of the two Caribbean outposts of Martinique and Guadeloupe as Overseas Departments. It is the economic incursions into Latin America that have come under the scrutiny of the PCF, whose journals are apt to cite endless lists of French mining, industrial, and banking firms operating in Brazil, Mexico, Chile, Peru, and Argentina. For example, Renault is at times singled out for its monopoly of automobile production in Colombia.

Martinique and Guadeloupe are, of course, special situations, and the PCF and PS both urge immediate self-determination. The Communists have also been critical of the large public aid program, which they see as a ruse to offset the huge payments deficits of these islands. Since the funds are used to finance French imports, the huge sums involved ultimately return to metropolitan France as private capital--thereby perpetuating the relationship of dependency.[31]

The PCF maintains effective ties with local communists on the islands.[32] In November 1976, a meeting was held in Paris between PCF leaders and corresponding leaders in the Departments (including Réunion). All sides called for a referendum on self-determination that would yield autonomy to the islands.

Chile. Events in Chile have received continued wide coverage in the PCF press. The collapse of the Popular Unity government, a trauma for the French Left as a whole, served as an object lesson, bringing into focus the vulnerabilities of the "peaceful transition to socialism" strategy. Here too, the PCF maintains ties with the Chilean party, although such relations are not of great significance, particularly after communist critics branded as a "sordid deal" the Soviet exchange of dissident Vladimir Bukovsky for Chilean Communist leader Luis Corvalan. The PS, too, has been much concerned with Chile and has carefully maintained its own links with the Popular Unity forces. Significantly enough, Mitterrand joined Allende's widow for a well-publicized Chilean Solidarity Conference in Paris in 1974, saying that Chile was an "important, original experiment: a socialism that respected public liberties."[33] The Socialists and Communists (as well as the French government) hosted Mrs. Allende again in 1977. All in all, both the PCF and the PS are agreed that France should halt all aid to the Pinochet government, particularly on the sale of arms. Accordingly, Giscard is criticized for such aid on the grounds that it is merely designed to open up Chile to penetration by French multinationals.

For the Socialists, Chile served to highlight their suspicions of the World Bank. In fact, they have long been critical of the IBRD as a manipulative organization in its loan and development policies. (This will be covered in more detail further on.) They point out that such manipulation was confirmed when, under Robert McNamara (and US pressure), the bank played a contributory role in financially isolating the Popular Unity government.[34]

Arms Sales to Third World Nations

Not surprisingly, the PCF is critical of French arms sales to various states around the world and no doubt would change existing policies considerably, given a government position enabling them to do so. On the one hand, these sales are seen as a device to offset France's deficits--a plausible argument considering the value of those sales: Fr20 billion in 1976. (The world's third largest supplier of weapons, France's 4 percent of the world's arms trade hardly compares, however, with US and Soviet sales.) On the other hand, these weapons are also attributed strategic value, in that they can help consolidate, in the party's view, reactionary regimes.

The PCF asserts that if it were in the government, it would cease the commerce in arms with all states that are fascist, racist, or aggressive. The party press has been especially outspoken about sales of French weapons to the Mobutu regime (later used against MPLA forces in Angola) and of sales (now generally ended) to South Africa. They have also opposed the substantial sales to Iran, Saudi Arabia, and Morocco. The Socialists are essentially in agreement in opposing these weapons sales, particularly to South Africa and Rhodesia.[35]

While there seems, therefore, to be a left-wing consensus on arms sales, it remains unclear whether, to what extent, or how quickly, a left-wing government in 1978 would have implemented such a policy. The Socialists, for example, have pointed out that approximately 100,000 wage earners in France are directly engaged in arms production for export and that wholesale dislocation of the export arms industry would lead to unemployment. A further unresolved issue is whether either (or both) of the left-wing parties would seek, as a government party, to furnish arms to those insurgent or liberation movements it favors.

The New Economic Order

The concept of a "new" world order in trade

83

and economic relations was originated by the Third
World states themselves, in their increasingly articulated demands at various North-South confrontations for a restructuring of these relations. The
French Socialists, we will see, have placed great
emphasis on the urgency of many of these demands.
Both left-wing parties have endorsed the view that
this new economic order represents the legitimate
and urgent aspirations of the Third World to in-
dustrialize and obtain access to technological
progress.

Yet some important differences in policy and
emphasis can be discerned. The Socialists have
tended to support various export stabilization programs established between EEC countries and the
Third World, while the Communists remain opposed,
in part because they reject the EEC as a proper
framework. These programs were initiated to stabilize certain economic conditions in the developing countries by reducing sharp fluctuations in raw
material prices of goods exported to Europe. But
the Communists make a counterargument: that they
are a device to assure a steady supply of raw materials to the EEC countries, and that they preserve the developing nations' subordinate economic
role of supplier of raw materials at low prices.
The PCF also maintains that these stabilization
programs have the subsidiary goal of preventing the
formation of new Third World cartels along the
model of OPEC.

The call for a new economic order, obviously,
is not a demand for immediate equality among all
nations, rich and poor. Rather, it is a desire to
countervail the overwhelming dependence that has
characterized the Third World's relationship to the
industrialized states. Since World War II and the
advent of the Bretton-Woods framework, the industrial states of the West have managed both the
rules and functioning of international economic
arrangements, despite de jure independence of the
LDC's. While the formal aspects of Western political domination collapsed with colonialism, the substantive aspect of this domination has persisted
into the era of decolonization: the so-called
neocolonial relationship.

THE SOCIALISTS AND THE THIRD WORLD

During the "belle epoque" of left-wing alliance in the mid-1970s, both the PS and PCF embraced

the Third World as part of a general "Mediterranean
temptation," a tendency to imagine the Union of
the Left as a national liberation movement and its
parliamentary-electoral battles as a national liberation struggle. As we have seen, the PCF argues
that many of the past accords reached between
France and various African states should be revised
because of clauses that restrict the sovereignty of
the developing states, imposed in negotiations that
were unequal during the period when these states
were just arriving at independent status. The PS
agrees that French state aid must be entirely disinterested, and seemed quite adamant in this radical view especially during the years of revolution
in Portugal, Greece, and Spain. In the past few
years, however, the PS's "Mediterranean temptation" has become less pronounced as it has developed greater "Northern" European ties, particularly
with the German SPD. The Communists were quick to
link this shift of focus with a general Socialist
party "turn to the right." In a simpler world this
might be believable. Here, as elsewhere, the Communists were free to "shoot from the hip" because,
as evidenced in 1977-1978, they were finally unwilling to go to government in a real world of limited possibilities. The Socialists, astride two
chairs since the alliance's inception in 1972,
again suffered the consequences. How the Socialists envisage France's relations to the developing
nations remains to be examined,[36] before drawing
conclusions concerning the French Left's Third
World policy as a whole.

In the PS analysis, the central problem for
the LDC's is that investment and financial decision making in the world is generally determined by
the developed nations. Because of this, the new
nations are forced to conform to an international
division of labor enforced to their detriment by an
exploitation of their natural resources. As a result, the modernized sectors of their economies are
largely shaped and controlled from abroad. Some of
the poorer developing states have become so totally
dependent upon the industrialized nations that they
are no longer in any way masters of their own development. For example, the need to import elabo-
rate technology from abroad forces them to acquire
foreign exchange. Hence, they must develop their
own exports and accept the establishment of foreign
firms on their soil. But the pattern of world
trade imposed by the dominant countries works in
the LDC's disfavor, forcing them to become suppliers of relatively simple commodities.

85

Then, too, there is the problem noted earlier
that non-oil producing Third World nations have become heavily saddled with foreign debt--an amount
which grew from $51 billion to $119 billion between
1967-1973 (rising at an annual rate of 15 percent).
By late 1977 the total debt was estimated at $180
billion, owed to other governments, commercial
banks, and leading international institutions. The
"Group of 77" LDC's has asked for a blanket cancellation of the $48 billion total owed to foreign
governments.

Debt service alone ($11 billion annually in
1973) compels these states to assign an ever-grow-
ing share of their export revenues merely to this
nonproductive burden, although the possibility of
major default appears to be significantly less severe today than a few years ago. At that time the
Socialists foresaw the possibility that the accumulated debt of these nations by 1980 could exceed
the net transfers made to the Third World: 'The
Third World states will be aiding the developed
states, an absurd situation,' their analysis noted.

As a first priority, then, the Socialists insist that steps be taken to lighten the burden of
this debt, which, of course, is one of the priority
demands of the LDC's themselves. With the rise in
debt, the Third World is demanding an equal increase in aid. Yet the more aid received in the
form of loans, the more their debt and dependency
increases.

France in 1975 contributed private and public
aid of Fr17 billion (1.17 percent of GNP). This,
however, includes Fr4.2 billion destined to the
Overseas Departments and territories (DOM-TOM).
France's public aid to the Third World in 1975 ran
at approximately .58 percent of GNP (.39 percent
without the DOM-TOM), well below the French government and UN goal of .7 percent. This aid chiefly
goes to states recently administered by France:
about 70 percent of it is destined for Africa.
Private aid, on the other hand, is more diversified:
only 36 percent of it goes to the French Zone and
North Africa. In other words, the Socialists argue,
French capitalism has a well-protected preserve in
Africa, yet it does not reject profit opportunities
in other areas, such as Latin America (a point
which, we saw, was noted by the Communists as well).

In a broad historical sense, the Socialists
concede that de Gaulle left behind a positive legacy in the eyes of the Third World, considering that
the major steps in decolonization occurred during

86

his presidency. Accordinqly, their chief criti-
cisms have been directed at President Giscard
d'Estaing, who has made French aid and development
more receptive to specifically French interests.
Like the Communists, therefore, the Socialists de-
plore a cultural assistance which encourages language and schoolinq under French methods in a way
that is reminiscent of the colonial era and which
is hardly adapted to the needs of modern Africa.
Similarly, they criticize aid programs which tie
Third World purchases of equipment to French enter-
prises, thereby making of aid a subsidy for French
exports, at the expense of the interests of the
beneficiary nations. Consequently, the PS generally concludes that France is not meeting her international obligations, and is losinq the goodwill
accumulated under de Gaulle.

Multilateral Aid

In theory, the French Socialists prefer this
form of aid. However, they offer varying evalua-
tions of the different world organizations which
administer it:

- The United Nations: The PS is essentially
  critical of UN performance to date. Not
  only is it weak, but it is far more political than it pretends. Since the United
  States is the chief supplier of funds, it
  has an inordinate voice in decision making.
- The World Bank: The Socialists are even
  more critical here. It imposes unreasonable
  conditions on Third World states and inter-
  feres in their internal affairs, as in
  Chile. The Socialists are also suspicious
  because it is dominated by capitalist
  states, and could well work against a French
  left-wing government.
- EEC: Here the Socialists are more tolerant.
  They approve of the association status accorded to African states at Yaoundé (and
  which was then extended to other states by
  the Lomé Convention in 1975). They also approve of the STABEX mechanism to protect
  against fluctuations in exports, and favor
  the duty exemptions given Third World exports
  enterinq EEC countries.

The Lomé accord is generally viewed by the PS
as a key innovation in relations between

underdeveloped and industrialized states, since it attempts to correct imbalances in these relations by giving the Third World nonreciprocal advantages on the export of its products to EEC nations. Nevertheless, according to the Socialists' analysis, Lomé does not respond fully to the requirements and demands of the new states. These countries seek long-term development agreements. What they genuinely require is a basic redistribution of world wealth, a redistribution not based on capitalist rules of international exchange which in the past have always led to their domination.

Capitalist and Socialist Development Models

Socialist analysis distinguishes between capitalist model and socialist model states. The former:

- are states such as South Korea, Singapore, and Brazil;
- tend to develop export goods economies;
- are wide open to multinationals;
- ignore the needs of their populations by developing a compradore class, fostering wide inequality.

Socialist model states are those such as Algeria, Cuba, and China. They seek more than mere increases in GNP: they are attempting to meet the broader aspirations of the great majority of their people. To attack the roots of misery, they will accept a less dramatic rate of growth.

Breakdown of the Economic Order

The Socialists argue that the capitalist world economic order is in major crisis. Economic liberalism, the laissez-faire rules of world trade as conceived at Bretton-Woods and further developed by GATT, along with the entire structure designed on postwar US hegemony, is weakening--perhaps even breaking down. A liberalism designed to prevent the narrow protectionism of the interwar years, it still signifies the old-world order to the Socialists. Several factors are now in operation, according to such analysis:

- the rise of Japan and Europe as powers in their own right;
- the loss of dominance by the US, particularly

88

with the "77" making broad challenges at
world forums;
- the US defeat in Vietnam;
- the <u>coup de grace</u> provided by the oil price
increases of 1974.

Given these developments, the Third World is
demanding new rules of the game. The old economic
order was postulated on unlimited access at cheap
prices to the world's natural resources. This is
now undermined, and the industrial nations are being compelled to negotiate. The OECD states in
particular are being confronted by an array of co-
alitions: the nonaligned countries of 1973, the
"Group of 77" at the UN, and the OPEC states. By
1975 these groups were potent enough to compel the
US to agree to a North-South dialogue. What is
more, they were strong enough to expand the agenda
beyond merely the energy crisis--so that the entire
question of equality could be approached (despite
US objections).

Such, then, is the Socialists' description of
the Third World confrontation. They are in essential agreement with LDC demands to restructure
the rules of international exchange. To stabilize
raw material prices, they have proposed a system
of buffer stocks, storing surplus produce to regu-
late the tensions between supply and demand. They
would further extend the policy of generalized
preferences (i.e., extend an already-existing EEC
mechanism), establishing a system of nonreciprocal
preferential tariffs to allow Third World nations
to export their manufactured goods to industrial
nations. They also propose some novel reforms of
the world monetary system, modifying the voting
system within the IMF, giving these countries a
larger decision-making voice.

In financing development aid, the Socialists
would emphasize public funding, and it would be
multilateral in nature, not bilateral. This would
preclude the donors using it as a means of influ-
encing the beneficiaries. Furthermore, the Socialists are obviously well disposed toward the Canadi-
an and Swedish decisions to write off $254 million
and $200 million, respectively, in LDC debts.
While the PS would probably refuse the notion of a
blanket cancellation, they would go further in the
practice of case-by-case write offs than do the
present French and other Western governments, by
considering the write off of certain whole cate-
gories of debts, or the debts of certain groups of

countries. The PS might even accept a debt mora-
torium (Mitterrand's 1974 presidential program
called for a "study" of this question). The Socialists are also proposing an unusual (and utopian)
system of communal ownership of unexplored territories, such as ocean explorations. Profits would
be used to finance Third World development. And
finally, they set as a goal for France the achievement of a rate of public aid at .7 percent of
GNP.[37]

CONCLUSION

     The Left historically has identified itself in
France as the party of social justice. Popular
opinion has generally concurred. Whether or not
the left-wing parties would have implemented a
"socialist" policy in relations with the Third
World, or will ever do so, the Left's discourse on
problems of underdevelopment derives from a profound and authentic tradition of identification
with the disadvantaged and the oppressed. Despite
General de Gaulle's unique popularity in Third
World nations, and aided by the Right's historical
record of rigid pursuit of self-interest, socialism
has successfully claimed as its own the tradition
of social generosity within the French political
culture. Yet traditions eventually die, or at
least weaken if they are not reinforced with enthusiasm inspired in the quotidian. In considering
whether the Left's traditions in Third World policy are being invigorated still today, certain differences distinguish the Socialist and Communist
Parties, differences in élan which seem congruent
with a more general pattern.
     Over the past decade, the PCF leadership has be-
gun in important ways to move away from its traditional attitudes of political abstention and rejection. The recent and grudging provisional acceptance
of France's nuclear defense arsenal and of direct
elections to the European parliament, for example,
are signs of a new policy approach, issuing from reluctant agreement with an Italian Communist realization that abstainers are generally losers. This
"participationist" inclination--the will to be part
of a debate even when one is not sure or even likely to win--has not yet, however, affected PCF discourse on the developing nations. Here the French
Communists tend still to speak more as Soviet loyalists, Stalinist permanent oppositionists, than as

Eurocommunists. They continue to harp on a unilateralist dramaturgy of national liberation from monopoly capitalist imperialism rather than expounding the less demonological, but more real dilemmas of improved trade, aid, and redistribution among unequal but not irreconcilable states. As with its old policy on nationalizations (nationalizations done without the PCF were "statist" and not "socialist," therefore to be opposed), the French Communists' Third World discourse remains basically prophylactic: its purpose is to prevent, or at least oppose and discredit any policy for development which promises to integrate Third World countries more thoroughly with Western institutions. For this reason, the PCF has rejected the French-sponsored "North-South dialogue" from the beginning, arguing that the only possible outcome was a new series of "unequal treaties" imposed because of a given relation of forces in world politics. The PCF is thus at least faithful to its own doctrine in its preference for bilateral over multilateral aid, the UN to the European Community/Atlantic/North-South frameworks.

The French Socialists, historically participationist, have been in their recent anticapitalist resurgence, more attracted by Italian than French Communist attitudes. They propose to join the system and to work for its change from within. Their policy is for France to act in North-South relations as "an element of contradiction among the industrialized countries and a supporter and friendly critic of Third World demands." While at certain times, in certain forums, and with certain Socialists, this desire can be presented in a more or less Leninist-sounding theory of capitalist imperialism, the Socialists generally speak from a less unilateral view of international inequalities and exploitation. The PS policy here is thus like the PS view of the European Community--it accepts that a political price must be paid for access to the real centers of decision making. The Socialists have been therefore must more interested in the North-South dialogue than the PCF and have been equally less interested in committing the party unequivocally and in violent language to a given movement of insurrection, secession, or invasion. (An interesting foreshadowing of PS government behavior toward the Third World is the fact that Claude Cheysson, a well-known European Community commissioner with close ties to the PS and who was mentioned as a possible foreign minister in a

91

Mitterrand government, had a large role in negotiating the EEC's STABEX commitments.)

Thus, Third World policy in the left-wing alliance was several things at once. First, it was necessary. The projet de société and global "five-year contract for government" strategy of the French Left, which like the Napoleonic Code was an encyclopedia of the subject, required a solution to every problem, or at least a proposal consistent with the idea of a "transition to socialism."

Second, policy toward the developing nations was an area of comparatively easy agreement between otherwise seriously divided Socialists and Communists, primarily because of its highly hypothetical character. Such decisions would not be the first order of business of a left-wing government. Given this, certain sweeping radical promises would have to be faced realistically only after (i.e., if) other more immediate and ominous dilemmas were resolved.

Third, a radical left-wing alliance Third World policy was a signal, convincing or not, of the Left's combativeness. Symbolically, an unambiguous anti-imperialist Third World policy made the Union of the Left into a sort of national liberation movement in its home country. While electoral benefits were not necessarily obvious (a left-wing party was not likely to win many votes in Pas-de-Calais by promising more development aid to Chad or to close a naval base off Madagascar, and it would likely lose votes in certain agricultural areas by espousing special access to the French market for Third World foodstuffs), the mobilizing effect on the Left's rank-and-file of consistent international, as well as national anticapitalism, seemed not negligible. Such a policy could combine enthusiasm for diverse revolutionary movements in Chile, Indochina, Portugal, and in the former Portuguese African possessions of Angola and Mozambique--a useful combination in domestic politics, if not internationally. At the least, one sees easily that a more measured and internally disputed left-wing Third World policy could have had a demobilizing effect.

Fourth, and in summary, one sees retrospectively that the uses or functions of Third World policy were significant basically only in relation to the French Left's internal politics. In retrospect, the French Left's Third World policy had relatively little to do either with policy or the Third World.

For the Communist Party, a rigid and unilateralist Third World policy (which, in cases of a disagreement with the PS, the Common Program ignored
rather than rejected) served a function of ideological or symbolic integrity. In the face of several
"Eurocommunist" compromises elsewhere in party policy, a totally unambiguous "two-camp" theory of international relations was one way for the Communists to say metaphorically, "We haven't really
changed, we are still revolutionaries and communists." While this may not have been necessarily
helpful in domestic relations with non-Communists,
the PCF leaders during the Union of the Left alliance persistently had to show equal concern with
Eurocommunizing the party's image and with maintaining its identity. After all, a left-wing convergence in France at some point raises the question of whether there really remains anything very
distinctive about the Communist Party. Yet, while
Georges Marchais is no doubt much less interested
in the theme of reconsolidating the historic split
of the European Left than is Santiago Carrillo or
even Enrico Berlinguer, the fact that the Communists were consistently most dogmatic in areas
somewhat peripheral to the left-wing program was a
point of comparison which provided non-Communist
observers a certain perspective on Communist purpose elsewhere, at least until the PCF began to up
the stakes ideologically in 1977 during the negotiations for updating the program's core policies.
     An unambiguous anticapitalist Third World
policy also had a function of ideological coherence
for the Socialists. To become an "element of contradiction among the industrialized countries" in
this sense had dual usefulness. On the one hand,
it could serve to legitimize the PS's new identity
as a committed socialist party; on the other, it
repudiated the Socialists' discredited heritage on
the problem of decolonization--i.e., it set the PS
off distinctly from the SFIO and set François Mitterrand off from his own past record. Mitterrand
made a considerable effort in the middle 1970s to
forge strong links with Mediterranean socialist
parties and leaders, both in Europe (e.g., Mario
Soares, Felipé Gonzalez, and Andreas Papandreou)
and in Africa (especially with Leopold Senghor). In
1975 Mitterrand took the initiative for a meeting
of Southern European socialist leaders in France,
a symbolic disengagement from his own Algerian policy as minister of the interior during the Fourth
Republic. Finally, similar to the PS-PCF relation

93

as a whole, the majority-minority relation within
the Socialist Party itself—the relation between
the Mitterrand majority and the left-wing CERES
minority—found a point of unity in elaborating
Third World policy. The CERES was hard put to out-
bid the majority's Third World policy.

All things considered, it is doubtful that the
PCF has been able to achieve among its militants
more than a stagnant, increasingly burdensome, and
artificial enthusiasm for anti-imperialism. To be
sure, the party apparatus continues to produce
manichaean analyses of Third World problems, as of
international relations generally, with a breadth
and detail that unfailingly recalls the traditional
Communist Party pretension to understand the world
in its entirety and its complexity—a hope which
the Communists have succeeded in bureaucratizing
along with so much else. The PCF monthly Cahiers
du Communisme, the weekly La Nouvelle Critique and
other more specialized publications continue to
churn out a stultifying amount of print. The Central Committee staff work for a "shadow government," one might say. Yet it is at bottom still a
rhetoric of permanent opposition, consonant with
the party leadership's turn away from a real chance
at government in 1977-1978. Furthermore, one
wonders whether the PCF's rank-and-file is much
moved any longer by simplistic notions of the international communist movement's purity in relations with the Third World. Surely the Soviet
Union has compromised itself too obviously in recent years, as in the Ogaden imbroglio, and the
general degradation of the Soviet Union's image in
the French Communist movement cannot but further
weaken the belief in a Third World policy of revolutionary internationalism.

Beginning with the Socialists' renaissance in
1969-1971, one suspects that it was they who in the
past decade successfully touched hands again with
the Left's traditional identification with the oppressed. A more efficient use of world resources
and significant transfers of technology to developing countries might be acts of enlightened self-
interest, as the Socialists have alleged. Yet
their advocacy of a "new international economic
order" resonates first of all as a call for justice.
The Communists, to be sure, have also framed some
of their proposals in terms of France's self-
interest. Indeed, the Communists' traditional pro-
ductivism and new nationalism may find such arguments increasingly more pertinent, but in the

meantime the Socialist leadership, with its human-
ist discourse, seems the more genuine French Left.

The "Mediterranean temptation" of the Socialist Party seems largely to be over today, given the
collapse of the Union of the Left and the conservative trends issuing from the Portuguese and
Spanish revolutions. Nonetheless, even the PS's
recent turn to closer ties with the SPD is not certain to quiet American anxieties about Socialist
Party foreign policy in general, nor about its
Third World policy in particular. To the extent
that in relations with the developing countries
West European and American interests diverge--and
they do in some significant respects--the PS turn
"North" may not resolve the American policy problem, but merely change it. To the extent the
Yaoundé-Lomé pattern of EEC-Third World nation
agreements is continued--a policy which the Socialist Party supports--a network of privileged relations would be established between Western Europe
and the developing nations from which the United
States would be excluded, or only very selectively
admitted. Unexpectedly, one sees the way in which
a less doctrinaire but more influential Socialist
Party could be truer to itself. If the Communist
Party were to catch the echo, the French Left's
future might begin to seem again not quite so
pointless.

NOTES

1. Programme commun de gouvernement du Parti
communiste et du Parti socialiste (Paris: Editions
sociales, 1972), Part IV, especially pp. 183-85.
PCF texts relative to the 1977 failure to agree on
an updated program are: Programme commun de gouvernement actualisé (Paris: Editions sociales,
1978) and Pierre Juquin, Programme commun: L'actu-
alisation a dossiers ouverts (Paris: Editions
sociales, 1977).
2. Each party had its own reaction to the
1975 Lomé Agreement, following on Yaoundé II three
years after the Common Program was drafted.
3. Fernando Claudin, The Communist Movement
from Comintern to Cominform (New York: Monthly Review Press, 1975), Vol. II, pp. 336-37.
4. Ibid., p. 338.
5. In evaluating the two parties, it is less
easy to speak of a specific Socialist Party line
on the Third World since the party has traditionally

operated within a pluralistic framework where factions are free to form. Thus, strong groupings
within the party would oppose this or that policy,
often transforming political virtue into party in-
coherence. Many who had a falling out on the Algerian question would later join with Mendès-France
in forming the PSU in 1958-1959.

6. Even when relations have been less acri-
monious than today, the PCF has been quick to cite
the Socialist Party role in various past wars, dem-
onstrating that the latter has been historically
hostile to liberation movements. See e.g., L'impérialisme français aujourd'hui (Paris: Editions
sociales, 1976), an edited collection by the PCF
Central Committee Foreign Policy section.

7. The Socialists have evoked an especially
symbolic historical parallel, comparing Third World
demands for a new economic order with the nine-
teenth century struggle of European workers to form
unions to win their rights. See Lionel Jospin, ed.,
Les Socialistes et le Tiers Monde (Paris: Berger-
Levrault, 1977), p. 120.

8. Changer la vie: Programme de gouvernement
du Parti socialiste (Paris: Flammarion, 1972),
pp. 193-97. The PCF program, referred to below, is
Programme pour un gouvernement démocratique d'union
populaire (Paris: Editions sociales, 1971).

9. L'impérialisme français, op.cit. Much of
this is based on Martin Verlet's essay, pp. 11-33.

10. Ibid., p. 14.

11. Ibid., p. 28.

12. This does not mean the PCF supports every
savage act of the liberation struggle. For example, the PCF Central Committee condemned the kill-
ings at the 1972 Munich Olympics as an adventurist
act which "ill-served the just cause of the Pales-
tinian Arabs." See Cahiers du Communisme, October
1972, pp. 127-28.

13. It is important to note that neither the
Communists nor the Socialists view the Third World
as a homogeneous "interest group." They carefully
distinguish between states that have chosen capitalist or socialist paths to development.

14. Cahiers du Communisme, July-August 1977.

15. L'impérialisme français, pp. 39-40. In
general, the PCF would like to see the socialist
bloc more aggressive in world politics, and has
criticized Soviet moderation in this regard (in
particular, during preparatory meetings for the
1976 East Berlin conference).

16. South Africa's de Beers now has

prospecting rights on the island, Japan has secured
fishing rights off the island, and West Germany has
investments there, since Madagascar is one of the
Associated States linked to EEC. (The PCF, inci-
dentally, has shown particular sensitivity to the
SPD's links to the social democrats on that island.)

17. L'Humanité, April 5, 1976, p. 2.
18. Ibid.
19. Ibid., p. 2.
20. Before the Somali eviction of Soviet influence, the PCF had not taken sides publicly in
the struggle over the Ogaden area. Generally, the
PCF follows the Soviet line, which holds that colonialism's legacy carved out arbitrary territorial
entities in Africa, bearing little relationship to
actual ethnic or tribal divisions. This condemns
Third World nations to endless national disputes
following their independence, such as in the Niger-
ian Civil War or the Somalia situation.
21. See the analysis by Michel Charlot in
L'Impérialisme français, p. 65.
22. Cahiers du Communisme, July-August 1972,
pp. 63-78.
23. See Ferenc Vali, Politics of the Indian
Ocean Region (New York: MacMillan, 1976). He
notes that US submarines operating in the Indian
Ocean are within easy missile range of European
Russia.
24. See Jacques Couland in L'Impérialisme français, p. 6. On the general character of France's
energy policy, see Horst Mendershausen, Coping with
the Oil Crisis: French and German Experiences (Bal-
timore: Johns Hopkins University Press, 1976); Guy
de Carmoy, Energy for Europe: Political and Economic Implications (Washington, D.C.: American Enterprise Institute, 1977); Robert J. Lieber, Oil
and the Middle East War: Europe in the Energy Crisis (Cambridge, Mass.: Harvard Center for International Affairs, 1976), and "Energy Policies of the
Fifth Republic," paper presented to the Conference
on the Impact of the Fifth Republic on France, SUNY
(Brockport, N.Y.), June 9-11, 1978.
25. However, see Bernard J. Crescenzo's essay
"Quelle politique energétique pour la France?" in
L'Impérialisme français. He does suggest that cooperation with the East bloc could provide France
with natural gas and coal.
26. Robert Lambotte, "L'Algérie dix ans après
l'indépendance," Cahiers du Communisme, October
1972, pp. 88-98.
27. L'Humanité, September 12-16, 1974.

28. PCF links to Third World movements and governments were quite active at that time. Earlier that year Marchais journeyed to Hanoi to invoke a "world front" against imperialism.

29. L'Humanité, April 7, 1977, p. 7. The PCF foreign policy spokesman Jean Kanapa was in Algeria earlier in 1977, and later in the year held talks in Libya, one result of which was reported to be coordinated diplomatic initiatives in support of the Palestinians. One may speculate that the PCF's active Mediterranean diplomacy at this point was not entirely foreign to Soviet intentions in the same area, the Horn and the Middle East.

30. Giscard d'Estaing sought to justify his policy by describing the venture as an act on behalf of "Europe." L'Humanité pointed out that not all European states supported the venture, nor had any been consulted. There is a slight irony here: had Giscard actually consulted NATO or the European Council, the Communists probably would have been the loudest to complain, citing it as further evidence that Giscard had mortgaged French sovereignty. For details on the Communist reaction, see L'Humanité of April 1, 4, 9, and 11, 1977.

31. Cahiers du Communisme, January 1977, p. 121. Also, see L'Impérialisme français, pp. 153-54.

32. The PCF also maintains quite active party ties with its Cuban counterparts. In addition, Marchais recently has spent winter vacations there.

33. L'Humanité, July 8, 1974, p. 1.

34. Les Socialistes et le Tiers Monde, pp. 89-90.

35. See ibid., p. 173.

36. Much of the following is based on Les Socialistes et le Tiers Monde.

37. The 1972 PS program called for a 1 percent level made up entirely of public aid of a "totally disinterested" nature.

5
The French Communist Party, Polycentric Eurocommunism, and Eastern Europe

Pavel Machala

In the parliamentary elections held in France in March 1978, the leftist parties were defeated--though only by a very narrow popular margin.[1] It is a general assessment that the main reason behind this defeat was the partial breakdown of the leftist alliance, for which the French Communist party (PCF) was primarily responsible. Both the breakdown of the Communist-Socialist alliance and its subsequent defeat in these legislative elections came as a great relief to France's European allies and to Washington. Their relief was understandable for, correctly or not, they believed that Communist participation would have had serious consequences for the Atlantic Alliance. Furthermore, they believed that the victory of the leftist coalition in France would have created a psychological climate which would encourage similar domestic alignments in some other Western European countries, namely in Italy and Spain.

Odd as it may seem at first glance, the Soviet and the Eastern European reaction to the French electoral results suggests that these governments too were relieved by the leftist defeat. In analyzing the electoral results, the Soviet Communist party daily, Pravda, was quick to point out that V. Giscard d'Estaing, in his postelection speech, stated that "in the field of foreign policy, France will continue its course of independence, security, and peace."[2] Moscow was well aware of the fact that the ascension to power of a left-wing government in France could have jeopardized its already fragile relations with Washington, without any guarantee of improved relations with a new left-wing government to counterbalance this effect.

Ironically enough, Moscow seems to have developed much more relaxed relations with Giscard

d'Estaing's government than it has with the French
Communists, let alone with the Socialists. Just
prior to the French elections in March, the Soviet
foreign policy weekly, Za rubezhom, stated that
"the outcome of the National Assembly elections is
of importance not only for the situation inside the
country" but that "it will also exert a definite
influence on France's foreign policy." At the same
time, it pointedly added that, whereas the present
government "pursues the policy of national independence and supports international détente" and
"cooperation with the Soviet Union and the other
socialist countries," the Socialist party "pursues
the U.S. line" as well as that of the "Socialist
International, whose line is not always friendly
towards the socialist countries."[3]

In her mistrust of Communist participation in
the French government, Moscow, thus, seems to be
differentiating between the situation in France and
in Italy. She has supported the demands of the
Italian Communists for a governmental alliance with
the Christian Democrats because, from the Soviet
point of view, such participation would most likely
weaken NATO, but not so much as to endanger détente; furthermore, it would probably not lead to
any radical domestic changes and thus, would serve
to discredit Eurocommunism ideologically. On the
other hand, Moscow has opposed Communist participation in the left-wing government of France for precisely the same reasons that she would welcome such
participation in Italy. She believes that while
the participation of the Italian Communist Party
(PCI) would have little effect on the domestic situation in Italy, in France the participation of the
PCF would most likely have produced major social
and economic changes--changes that Moscow could not
have welcomed, both for pragmatic and ideological
reasons. Besides endangering détente, a Socialist-
Communist victory could have had a negative effect
on the French economy, the repercussion of which
would have been felt in the Soviet economy because
of important trade relations between the two countries. Furthermore, a leftist government could
have been expected to experiment with a form of
"democratic socialism" which would have represented
an ideological challenge to the Soviet and Eastern
European experience. In addition, the ascension to
power of such a left-wing government in France
could have forced the PCF into criticizing the
Soviet model of socialism, as yet articulated
fully only by the Spanish Communist party (PCE).

Such a critique could have put a strain on both the domestic and bloc stability of Eastern Europe, encouraging liberal dissent on the one hand, and the assumption of autonomistic positions by some Eastern European regimes on the other. Thus, the Soviet leaders have an interest in preventing the spread of this "Eurocommunist infection" to Eastern Europe and to the Soviet Union. They therefore expect to benefit from the leftist defeat in France in two ways: (1) détente will be preserved and its consequent economic benefits retained; and (2) the influence of Eurocommunism on Eastern Europe will be diminished.

It is my view, however, that both the West and the Soviet Union are deceiving themselves in their analysis of the effects of the recent French elections. It is an open secret that the PCF is the least liberal of all the major Eurocommunist parties. Its participation in the French government, far from paving the way for other Eurocommunist parties' participation in Western European governments, could actually hamper their chances. Conversely, if the PCF is kept out of the French government, this could very well enhance the chances of those more liberal Eurocommunist parties for legitimizing their claim to become part of a ruling coalition in their respective countries.

Although the rupture within the French Left has destroyed the possibility of the PCF's participation in the French government, it has not undermined the coalition strategy of the Communist parties in Italy and Spain. It has merely forced the latter two Eurocommunist parties to put some distance between themselves and the PCF, and to make every effort to strengthen friendly relations with Western Europe's socialist parties--including that of France. In Italy, this approach has evidently worked, for the local socialist party has been supporting the PCI's demand for a formal governmental role. Thus, paradoxically, rather than making Western Europe safe for liberal democracy, the failure of the French Communist party to sustain a unified relationship with other French leftist parties in the long run may be making Western Europe safe for Eurocommunism.

Soviet satisfaction with the results of the French parliamentary elections is based on a similar fallacy. The Soviets may be right in assuming that the rigidity of the PCF position as manifested during the elections reflects not only the tactical, but also the ideological gap between the three

101

major Eurocommunist parties. However, they are mistaken when they assume that this polycentric Eurocommunism is less dangerous as far as their own interests are concerned than monocentric Eurocommunism would be.

This essay will try to show that the destabilizing impact of Eurocommunism on Eastern Europe (both for domestic and bloc relations) will, in fact, be greater if the present polycentrism of that phenomenon is preserved.

POLYCENTRIC EUROCOMMUNISM

Before we can analyze the impact of Eurocommunism on the Eastern bloc, we must first define the meaning, and then define the mode of existence of this phenomenon. Some writers have reduced Eurocommunism to a one-dimensional concept, equating it with the mere independence of a given Communist party vis-à-vis the Soviet Union; such a formulation makes the Yugoslavs not only the candidates for, but the apostles of this doctrine. Others have gone to the opposite extreme, reducing its "ideal type"--to use Weberian jargon--into mere social democracy. Curiously enough, the most explicit, yet succinct definition of Eurocommunism was given by Santiago Carrillo, the General Secretary of the Spanish Communist party (PCE) in a Newsweek interview on January 24, 1977:

> By Eurocommunism, we mean independence from the Soviet Union and the socialist bloc of nations. We believe that socialism can't be the work of a single party, that the state can't be a party-state, or as it is often called, a "work-peasant" state. The state must be secular, without an official philosophy, [must] belong not to a party but to the society, and it must maintain all the collective and individual freedoms that now exist. The march to socialism must be the result of a consensus of the country's majority, and it must be submitted to regular electoral control, including government changes and all the characteristics of a democratic system. (my emphasis)

According to this definition, Eurocommunism has both a political and an ideological dimension. Although the rejection of Moscow's tutelage in both political and ideological matters is one of its

102

necessary characteristics, this alone does not make
a Eurocommunist party. Only the analysis of its
substantive position towards (1) the domestic political system; (2) regional integration and defense;
(3) the situation in the Eastern bloc countries;
and (4) the nature of the international communist
movement, can determine whether a given communist
party is Eurocommunist or not. Therefore, as a
political concept, Eurocommunism refers to the unconditional acceptance of civil liberties and the
multiparty system, the conditional acceptance of
the military division of Europe, commitment to
Western Europe's political unity, opposition to the
Kremlin's control of Eastern Europe, and criticism
of governmental oppression in the Eastern bloc.
As an ideological concept, Eurocommunism refers to
the development of a democratic "model" not only
for the transitional period, but also for the socialist society which is to follow. The Eurocommunists renounce the Leninist maxim which lays claim
to the privileged position for the communist party,
and thus, Eurocommunism as a doctrine guarantees
the preservation of political and ideological plu-
ralism. Ideologically, therefore, it represents
the "withering away" of "Leninism" and its replacement with a pluralistic, but economically and soci-
ally radical democracy. In sum, on the level of
ideology, Eurocommunism presupposes a total rupture
with the Soviet bloc.
     This, however, should not be interpreted to
mean that Eurocommunism is being transformed into
"social democracy," for the ultimate goal of all
Eurocommunist parties--even the most "liberal"
ones--is the socialist "transformation" of their
societies. In line with this is the implicit claim
that today, Eurocommunism remains the only true ex-
ponent of "creative Marxism." Therefore, rather
than describe Eurocommunism as "Marxism-Leninism
minus the dogmatic substance of Leninism" as some
writers have done, it may be more accurate to identify this phenomenon with the re-Europeanization of
revolutionary socialism.
     This being the case, the ideological signifi-
cance of Eurocommunism can, theoretically, take one
of two forms: (1) Eurocommunism can be viewed as a
model of socialist society that is applicable only
in an advanced capitalist setting; or (2) it can be
understood as an experience that claims a basic
superiority over any and all existing forms of socialism. As such, Eurocommunism can evolve not
only into a regional ideological and strategic

center, but also into the ideological heart of the
entire international communist movement. By "strategic center," I do not mean an "organizational center," i.e., one which directs the national policies
of the individual Western European communist parties. What I mean by this term is a center in
which these parties discuss and coordinate policies
pertaining to the European Community.

When understood in this way, it becomes evident that in practice Eurocommunism as such does
not exist as a full-blown phenomenon: it is not
embraced totally in any or all of its aspects by
any of the Western Communist parties that--explicit-
ly or implicitly--consider themselves Eurocommunist.
None of these parties has yet abolished "democratic
centralism" and allowed organized internal dissent.
The PCE has come the closest to de-Leninizing its
internal party structure not only by removing the
term "Leninism" from its statutes, or by allowing
the creating of regional party organizations, but
also by experimenting with a degree of internal
democracy. For example, at the PCE Congress that
was held in the spring of 1978, not only were mul-
tiple candidates on the ballot, but voting was also
secret.[4] In this, as in some other respects, the
Italian Communists are now lagging behind the Spanish, while remaining ahead of the French
Communists.

Nor is Eurocommunism simply a spectrum that
consists of parties of a more or less Eurocommunist
persuasion. Being a multidimensional phenomenon--
i.e., referring not only to independence vis-à-vis
Moscow in domestic and regional policies, but also
to the creation of an alternate "model" of a transitional and a socialist society--each Eurocommunist
party can and often does find itself holding a position of different intensity on different Eurocommunist issues. Finally, Eurocommunism historically
began not as a regional but as a national phenomenon, thus, at least initially, making differences
among the Eurocommunist parties inevitable. Among
other things, diverse domestic political and social
conditions together with differences in the social
composition of the parties' membership and personal-
ity differences of the top leadership in each party
must account for the uneven and intermittent development of the Eurocommunist mentality.

This conclusion might leave the impression that
there is not yet any minimum common ground among the
Eurocommunist parties other than their declared
independence vis-à-vis the Soviet Union and their

criticism of political repression in the Eastern
bloc. Such, however, is not the case. All the major Eurocommunist parties, for example, have declared themselves in favor of their countries' present defense alliances. Similarly, they have all
accepted adherence to the multiparty system during
the transition to socialism and the necessity of
political alliances with non-Communist forces. The
latter is true even with regard to the PCF, which,
despite its recent maneuvering, has not repudiated
the idea of a "Common Program" with the Socialists.

Beyond this minimum common denominator though,
one can detect two dominant ideological tendencies
in the Eurocommunist movement: (1) nationalism;
and (2) democratization. The first is typified by
the position of the French Communists, the second
by the Italians and the Spaniards, although there
remain important differences between the latter two
parties. In the Eastern European context, these
two trends have so far remained mutually exclusive,
as the experience of contemporary Hungary and Romania proves. However, in the Western European
context, both the "socialisme aux couleurs de la
France" and the "compromesso storico" presuppose
some dosage of both "autonomism" and "revisionism."
The difference between "nationalistic" Eurocommunism and "democratic" Eurocommunism is merely in
degree and not in kind. Hence, the existence of
Eurocommunism, but a Eurocommunism that is ideologically bicentric.

Furthermore, despite the fairly regular bilateral and multilateral meetings of the Eurocommunist
parties, there is not any immediate likelihood of
the emergence of either a regional or subregional
strategic center for the Eurocommunist movement.
Although on the surface the relations among the major Eurocommunist parties seem quite close, beneath
the surface there is evidence of continuous tension
due to different views pertaining to (1) their relations with the Soviet Union; (2) the character of
the political regimes in the Eastern bloc; (3) the
function of NATO; and (4) the nature of the "transitional" society in Western Europe.

So far, both the PCI and the PCF have refused
to consider anything approaching a political rupture with Moscow. However, there are still a number of differences between the two parties in their
approach to the Soviet Union. Whereas the Italians
try to avoid any unnecessary abrasiveness in their
relations with Moscow, the French, by contrast,
seem to enjoy occasional strains. On the other

hand, judging from the behavior of the PCE, the latter would not view a "formal break" as an unmitigat-
ed catastrophe. Similarly, the Italians and to a
lesser degree the French, are ready to level dis-
sociative criticism at the political repression and
lack of liberties in the Eastern bloc countries, but
they do not go along with the position of the Spaniards that none of these countries can be considered
a "workers' democracy."

    As far as their view on the nature of the
"transitional"--i.e., postcapitalist Western
Europe--is concerned, the Italian and the Spanish
Communist leaders foresee a permanent rapprochement
and convergence between Eurocommunism and Eurosocialism. Thus, for example, Enrico Berlinguer, the
head of the PCI, insists that although the term
"Eurocommunism" does not make sense as designating
a new international organizational center of "some
Communist parties in Western Europe," it does make
sense if one means by it the striving of the Western
European communist parties for political and philo-
sophical unity within the workers' movement of
Western Europe.[5] The PCF, on the other hand, continues to conceptualize the "transitional" period
as one characterized by the ideological struggle between Eurocommunism and Eurosocialism. It is obvious that different political realities in individual
Western European countries have served to encourage
the preservation of these individual strategic--and
to a lesser degree ideological--Eurocommunist centers in Rome, Paris, and Madrid.

THE FRENCH COMMUNIST PARTY AND EUROCOMMUNISM

    The historical evolution of the PCF's present
political position can only be described as "revolutionary." Since the "grand tournant" that was in-
stitutionalized at the twenty-second party Congress
in February 1976, the French Communists have made
important progress on several Eurocommunist issues.
Formerly "loyalists," they have moved to an independent position vis-à-vis Moscow. This position
has found expression not only in their affirmed commitment to "liberal democratic" freedoms and in
their provocative criticism of political repression
in the Eastern bloc countries, but also in the reversal of their stand on France's nuclear program,
that is, when they decided, contrary to their former
policy, to support its continued existence.
    However, ideologically, the PCF has not yet

106

managed to break significantly out of its Leninist
shell. This is so despite its decision to replace
the doctrine of the "dictatorship of the proletariat" with that of a "union of the French people" in
the party program. It is important to emphasize
that this "union of the French people" is fundamentally different from both the "historic compromise" and a "government of democratic concentration"
as advocated by the PCI and the PCE respectively.
This is because of the different objectives behind
these doctrines. The main objective behind the
doctrine of both the Italian and the Spanish Communists has been to lessen the polarization in their
societies. Therefore, both of them have been eager
to go beyond a purely leftist coalition--this despite the fact that they risk losing some electoral
support. The main objective behind the PCF's doctrine of a "union of the French people," on the
other hand, has been to make the most out of class
conflict. A corollary to this is their insistence
on remaining not merely a major party in France,
but the major party of the French Left.[6]
     This ideological rigidity on the part of the
PCF certainly was the main reason behind the breakdown of the Socialist-Communist alliance. The
zero-hour decision of the PCF to cooperate with the
Socialists in the second round of the legislative
elections, was made because the Communists did not
want to be blamed for a leftist defeat or to preclude any future cooperation with the Socialists.
On the surface, the split was caused by a rather
peripheral dispute over such things as higher minimum salaries for workers, higher taxes for the af-
fluent, and the extent to which the French economy
should be nationalized. In addition to the already
agreed upon government take over of privately owned
banks and nine major industrial groupings, the Communists demanded the nationalization of 729 of the
big nine's subsidiaries, while the Socialists only
agreed to the nationalization of 290 of them.[7]
     In part, the PCF may have provoked the dispute
in a tactical attempt to stabilize its slackening
electoral support vis-à-vis the growing Socialist
party. The same reason may, in part, have been behind the Communists' demand for the right to veto
the policies of the expected left-wing government.
The PCF's insistence on getting the Socialists to
lock themselves into a new binding radical agreement may also have been due to the Communists'
fear that the Socialists could otherwise dump them
if the Left won the election, and instead make a

deal with the "centrist" parties to run the country.
However, the Communists' demands must have deeper
roots, for the above-mentioned reasons would not,
in themselves, have merited risking the electoral
defeat of all the leftist parties in the crucial
parliamentary elections which took place in March
1978. The only reasonable explanation for the break
seems to lie, therefore, in the Communists' unreadi-
ness to abandon their Leninist claim to a "leading
role." They preferred to see the "Leftist Union"
defeated rather than occupy a junior (subsidiary)
position in its victory. This stance ideologically
separates the PCF from the other major Eurocommunist
parties which have already rejected such a vanguard
role. To be fair, however, it must be recognized
that neither the PCI nor the PCE has been faced by
a challenge of a Socialist party of approximately
equal strength. In Italy, the Communists have long
been far stronger than the Socialists and have no
need to fear them as political rivals. In Spain,
the situation is actually reversed, with the Socialists much stronger in electoral terms than the Communists, so the latter have very little to lose and
much to gain by rejecting a vanguard role for
themselves and calling instead for a political
alliance with the Socialists.

As indicated, one substantive characteristic
of a Eurocommunist party is its relative political
and ideological moderation and a willingness to govern through a coalition with other parties, even
those which are not socialist. By suddenly breaking away from its Socialist ally, the PCF seems to
have rejected this notion. However, it would be
totally premature to conclude that the current "crisis of identity" of the PCF represents a regression
to its long-standing neo-Stalinist orthodoxy. At
most, it reflects the problems connected with the
suddenness of the PCF's Eurocommunist transforma-
tion--a situation not at all unusual for "late com-
ers," as, for example, shown by the experience of
the Czechoslovak Communists in 1968. Nor is there
any evidence that "the hand of Moscow" was responsible for the PCF's intransigence,[8] or that the
Kremlin "recommended" this course to the French
Communists.[9] To believe that the PCF's independence
is built on such fragile foundations is to misunder-
stand the nature of its autonomy. It is an open
secret that the major impetus behind the PCF's movement away from Soviet domination was the party's
recognition of Soviet hegemonic tendencies that con-
flicted with the PCF's "national" interests. The

PCF's opposition to the Common Market and its acceptance of the "frappe de force" should be understood in a similar nationalistic context. Yet, to identify the Eurocommunist position of the PCF as "Gaullocommunism" is rather misleading. Instead, the PCF's "Eurocommunism" can be better seen as a marriage between the Communist reformism of the "Prague Spring" and the Romanian nationalistic Communism, albeit in a Western context.[10]

POLYCENTRIC EUROCOMMUNISM AND EASTERN EUROPE

After repeated futile attempts to bring the situation in the Western European Communist movement under control, Moscow has resigned itself to the existence of Eurocommunism.[11] Despite their realization of the potential threat which Eurocommunism presents both to their hegemony in Eastern Europe and to the viability of the neo-Stalinist model of socialism in that region, the Soviets find themselves unable to deal with the phenomenon of Eurocommunism in any other way. At the Conference of the European communist parties in Berlin in June 1976, Moscow made three important concessions: (1) it formally renounced its leading role in the international communist movement; (2) it accepted the right of each communist party to search out and pursue an independent road to socialism; and (3) it acknowledged the possibility of a peaceful democratic transition to socialism in the advanced capitalist countries.[12]

At a first glance, there appears to be some evidence that these concessions are less than permanent. Moscow continues to deny the existence of Eurocommunism, maintaining that the term exists only as one of the tools of "Western imperialism." At the same time the Soviet press continues to insist on the leading role of the CPSU and the universality of the Soviet experience. However, further examination of such evidence shows Moscow's growing accommodation to Eurocommunism. For example, at the Soviet celebration of the October Revolution in 1977 not only was Enrico Berlinguer, the Secretary General of the PCI, allowed to deliver a speech in which he reiterated the basic Eurocommunist principles, but his speech was published in full in the main Soviet newspaper Pravda. Similarly, the Kremlin avoided any hostile polemics over the latest PCE Congress, at which the Spanish Communists formally committed themselves to the Eurocommunist ideals by deleting the term "Leninism" from their statutes. Instead, the Soviet leaders confined themselves to the claim that the Eurocommunist maxims did not represent anything new, and that, for example, "the ideas expressed at the PCE Congress about the peaceful road to revolution [socialism] are based on Leninism."[13]

The factors motivating such apparently drastic concessions are not difficult to discover. Although the dispute between the Eurocommunist parties and Moscow superficially resembles previous conflicts within the international communist movement (e.g., the Soviet disputes with the Yugoslav, Chinese, and Czechoslovak communist parties), the absence of traditional options like military intervention, economic blockade, or excommunication make the current dispute radically different. For one thing, the Eurocommunist parties are beyond the reach of the Brezhnev Doctrine because they are protected by NATO and are not part of the "socialist commonwealth." Moreover, they are protected from excommunication by the fact that without the Eurocommunist parties, the international communist movement would, at best, shrink into a regional phenomenon, consisting primarily of the Soviet bloc regimes. At worst, Soviet excommunication could give impetus to the creation of a rival international communist movement--a movement which could conceivably have a broader international base of support and appeal than their own.

In sum, condemnation of the Eurocommunist parties would, in all likelihood, split the European communist movement.[14] Condemnation of an individual Eurocommunist party could have similar results, for it could (as shown by the recent Soviet attack on the Spanish Communist Party) serve to rally the support of other Eurocommunist parties behind the potential victim of Soviet excommunication.[15] In either case, any excessive criticism of Eurocommunism on the part of the Soviet leaders would threaten the very existence of Soviet ideological legitimacy by forcing them to sever their ties with the international communist environment. Therefore, as hard as it may be for them, the Soviets are trying to live with Eurocommunism. By preserving their ties with individual Eurocommunist parties, they hope to curb their "autonomistic" and "revisionistic" excesses.

To this end, Moscow actively encourages the existence of polycentric tendencies in Eurocommunism. By emphasizing the differences between the

major Eurocommunist parties the Soviets seek to
prevent the formation of a Eurocommunist bloc. The
explosion of articles in the Soviet press emphasizing the gaps which separate the various Eurocommunist parties is but one example of this policy.

Similarly, the leaders of all Eastern European
regimes--including the Yugoslavs--believe the preservation of the polycentric tendencies of Eurocommunism to be in their own interests. Given the
substantive differences which exist among the regimes in this region, such general agreement among
them on the issue of Eurocommunism may sound curious
at the very least. However, upon closer examination, this uniformity of opinions is quite understandable. The conservative pro-Moscow Eastern
European regimes of Bulgaria, Czechoslovakia, and
East Germany share the Soviet's fear of Eurocommunism because they view all its features as threat-
ening to their own domestic and international legitimacy. Therefore, if they have to live with the
"spectre of Eurocommunism," they can do so only if
it remains disunited and weak (preferably with the
Eurocommunist parties out of power), and if all the
extremes of this phenomenon are prevented from developing. Any aggressive insistence on party independence and autonomy in the international Communist movement or any criticism of the domestic conditions in Eastern Europe can be tolerated by them
only so long as it remains improvised by the individual Eurocommunist parties and is not presented
as a joint position. Hence, they welcome the present polycentricity of Eurocommunism for the same
reasons as Moscow does.

If we can say that for the above Eastern European regimes polycentric Eurocommunism represents
the lesser of the two evils, then we can also say
that for the other regimes in this region it represents an optimum situation. Not only does the existence of Eurocommunism in its present form significantly increase their freedom of maneuverability
vis-à-vis the Soviet Union on either domestic issues
or foreign policy, but it also enables them, when
necessary, to shop selectively in the Eurocommunist
"market place" for suitable support. Either ideologically or politically unified Eurocommunism could
not possibly play such a role, for like Moscow,
these regimes believe that monocentric Eurocommunism
would necessarily lead to a rupture in the European
Communist movement. Such an eventuality would not
only preclude any alignment of the Eastern European
regimes with the Eurocommunists against the Soviet

111

Union, but could also undermine their own domestic
legitimacy. Hence their double preference for polycentric Eurocommunism: it brings maximum benefits
with minimum costs.

The specific attitude of each individual Eastern European regime towards Eurocommunism and its
relations with individual Eurocommunist parties has
been influenced by a variety of both internal and
external factors.[16] No uniformity has existed even
within the pro-Soviet group, for the Czech regime,
unlike that of East Germany and Bulgaria, has been
by far the most vociferous opponent of the Eurocommunist phenomenon. The constant avalanche of criticism of Eurocommunism in the Czechoslovak press,
however, should not be interpreted as an offensive
campaign to force the Western European communist
parties back in line, but merely as a desperate defensive measure. This is because unlike the Bulgarian or East German leaders, the Czechoslovak
leaders remain preoccupied with coping with a relatively large group of active supporters of the
principles of Eurocommunism--remnants of the
"Prague Spring." This problem, in turn, is further
exacerbated by the Eurocommunists' public denunci-
ations of the actions of the Czechoslovak regime
against these elements.[17] The Eurocommunists feel
that in order to legitimize their own conception
of socialism they have to criticize the regime of
the country which serves in the West as a constant
reminder of the Soviet presence in Eastern Europe.
The Spanish Communists have virtually gone so far
as to not recognize the Czechoslovak Communist party at all as a representative of Czechoslovak Communism. For example, unlike other Eastern bloc
parties, the Czech party did not obtain an invita-
tion to the April 1978 PCE Congress. In addition,
during 1978 all the Eurocommunist parties marked
the tenth anniversary of the advent of Alexander
Dubček to power by publishing interviews with a
number of his former colleagues, now in domestic
or foreign exile--thus, emphasizing their continued
support for the ideas of the "Prague Spring." In
sum, both the Eurocommunists and the Czechoslovak
leaders find themselves locked into a situation in
which each group feels it must criticize the other
in order to preserve its own legitimacy.

At the other end of the spectrum, the Yugoslavs feel they have to defend the Eurocommunist
parties against any Eastern European or Soviet criticism. They consider the existence of these parties
a highly positive development in the international

112

communist movement and in Western European regional
politics--a development that could, as they perceive it, strengthen Yugoslavia's political and
economic position in Europe. Eurocommunism epito-
mizes for them an essentially outwardly oriented
phenomenon--a struggle on the part of the Western
European communist parties against both the Soviet-
centered type of communism and the idea of a capitalist united Western Europe. Although the Yugoslavs view Eurocommunism as an ally in forestalling
any potential Soviet attempt to bring their country
under Soviet influence in the post-Tito era, they
do not conceal their fear that along with the international communist center in Moscow (which they do
not recognize as legitimate), another communist
center, this time in Western Europe, might appear.
As during the height of the Cold War, this would
again serve to isolate Yugoslavia politically in
Europe, a situation that the Yugoslav leaders are
naturally trying not to repeat. In addition, given
the Eurocommunists' views with regard to a pluralistic political system, any ideological homogeneity
among the Eurocommunist parties might also have a
detrimental effect on party authority in Yugoslavia,
for such homogeneity could only increase the domestic attraction for the Eurocommunist "model." In
this latter respect, the Yugoslavs share Soviet
bloc interests in preventing Eurocommunism from becoming a monolithic ideology.

In the range between the Czechoslovak regime
at one end of this spectrum fighting Eurocommunism,
and the Yugoslav regime at the opposite and supporting it, the other Eastern European regimes, on the
whole, have shown a reluctance to become deeply involved in the dispute. Their official thesis has
been that there are not any Eurocommunist parties.
It is not just the maverick Romanians and the reformist Poles and Hungarians who hold this view,
but also the pro-Soviet East Germans and Bulgarians.
When Todor Zhivkov in a December 1976 article which
was made much of in Western circles denounced Eurocommunism, it was not the actions of the Western
European communist parties which he attacked, but
merely the "concept" of Eurocommunism.[18] He argued
that this term was invented by bourgeois writers in
order to split the European communist movement. In
fact, when the Western European communist parties
themselves decided to adopt the term "Eurocommunism" in the spring of 1977, Bulgarian publications
actually dropped any reference to that "sensitive"
term. Even at the Prague conference of the

international communist journal, Problems of Peace and Socialism, in April 1977, the Bulgarian delegate omitted any mention of the term. This mystifying behavior on the part of the Bulgarians (and to a degree, of the East Germans as well) can only possibly be explained by their recognition that polycentric Eurocommunism does not represent any major threat to their own domestic legitimacy. Not being subject to the same degree of criticism by the Eurocommunists as the Czechoslovak regime has been, they simply do not think that it would be prudent on their part to launch any verbal assault on them and thereby encourage their unity. Significantly, unlike the Czechs, the Bulgarians and the East Germans continue to maintain regular contacts with both the PCI and the PCF. As recently as January 1978, the Italian Communists were in Berlin for talks with the East German leaders. During the same period a top Bulgarian party delegation was in Rome for a meeting with the Italian Communist leadership.[19]

The Romanians maintain a position close to that of the Yugoslavs vis-à-vis Eurocommunism. They welcome Eurocommunism essentially because of their own struggle against Moscow's supremacy in the international communist movement. What they particularly like about Eurocommunism are statements which describe it as "socialism in French colors," or as "a creative application of Marxism-Leninism to individual circumstances." During the past decade, Romania has cultivated close bilateral ties with the Western European communist parties. Relations with the three largest Eurocommunist parties (the PCI, the PCE, and the PCF) have become very cordial because the Eurocommunist parties, in contrast to their readiness to castigate similar failures in other Eastern European countries and in the Soviet Union, have generally refrained from criticizing the repressive and authoritarian aspects of the Romanian regime. Such ties--if not an overt alliance--were most visible at the conference of the European communist parties in Berlin in June 1976, where the Romanian delegation, together with the Yugoslavs, sided with the Eurocommunist parties.[20] The Romanians have been hoping that their ties to the Eurocommunist parties would convince Moscow of the need to follow an ever more cautious course towards this independent-minded member of "the socialist commonwealth."

However, such ties should not be viewed as being based on any ideological harmony with regard to

114

domestic policies between Romania and the Eurocommunists, but only on their mutual emphasis on independence vis-à-vis Moscow. On the level of "domestic" ideology, in fact, the gap between the two has
remained as wide, if not wider, than that between
the Eurocommunists and the conservative pro-Soviet
regimes of Eastern Europe. The Romanians are careful to always point out that the multiparty system
advocated by the Eurocommunists may be suitable
only for advanced Western societies and that such a
political structure should not be generalized. However, when the PCF abandoned the concept of the dictatorship of the proletariat because it was considered by them to be obsolete for French society, the
Romanians still lost no time in rejecting this departure from the strict tenets of Leninism despite
their acknowledgment that different rules may apply
in Western societies.[21] They reacted with similar
force to the PCE's removal of the term "Leninism"
from its party statutes, despite the old personal
ties between the Romanian leader, Ceausescu, and
Carrillo. As far as the Romanians were concerned,
in this instance, Eurocommunist "revisionism" had
simply gone too far, for such heresy they feared,
could not only have a destabilizing effect on the
domestic situation in Romania, but could also lead
to a split within the European communist movement.
If this were allowed to happen, Eurocommunism would
lose all its usefulness even for Romania; hence,
Romania's preference for polycentric Eurocommunism.

Somewhere between the Romanian and the Bulgar-
ian-East German positions towards Eurocommunism
lies that of the Poles and the Hungarians. Both of
these latter countries have been experimenting with
domestic reforms, though the Hungarians have gone
somewhat further. At the same time, however, both
regimes have remained close allies of the Soviet
Union in foreign and in bloc policies. Thus, their
attitude towards Eurocommunism is, of necessity,
very complicated. On the one hand, they have gingerly been advocating "reformist roads to socialism," which would seem to imply their enthusiasm
for the "specific roads" of the Italian, Spanish,
and French Communist parties; the existence of such
roads could only strengthen the legitimacy of their
own domestic policies in Soviet eyes.[22] On the
other hand, they are afraid that Eurocommunism
could result in the development of a new center for
these parties.

Thus, both the Polish and Hungarian leaders
welcome the Eurocommunists' persistence in

upholding a reformist road to socialism. However,
they oppose any features of Eurocommunism that
could lead to the development of a separate (or alternate) model of socialist society, for such a
Eurocommunist model could eventually result in the
establishment of communist centers in Moscow and in
the West, each side claiming its center to be the
true one. Kádár explicitly maintains that "today...
the Communist world movement has no center or leading party."[23] Similarly, Edward Geireck asserts that
the Marxist-Leninist ideology "is in a state of continuous development, in a continuous search for
ever better solutions to problems which exist and
are supplied by life."[24] Both leaders know very
well that, if a "split" were to occur, they
would have to take the Soviet side unconditionally.
For this and other reasons they naturally oppose
any developments that would lead to the unification
of the various prevailing types of "Eurocommunism."
Whereas the Poles hope to prevent unity among the
Eurocommunist parties by remaining neutral in any
Eurocommunist-Soviet disputes, the Hungarians hope
to accomplish the same by actively mediating any
differences.

Both the Polish and the Hungarian regimes have
developed close and frequent relations with the
French and Italian Communist parties[25]--this despite
the fact that the Poles have been criticized on a
number of occasions in the French and Italian party
papers for their treatment of dissidents.[26] Unlike
the other Eastern bloc regimes (including the Romanians), the Hungarians seem not to have any problems with the Eurocommunist rejection of the dictatorship of the proletariat. Instead, Kádár has re-
peatedly stressed in one way or another that "what
matters is the achievement of socialism--pluralistic
socialism or any other kind of socialism, with or
without the dictatorship of the proletariat."[27]
From this it follows that the threshold of toler-
ance for Eurocommunism in Hungary and Poland is
higher than it is in the rest of Eastern Europe
with the exception of Yugoslavia--but, there is a
threshold nonetheless.

This threshold was crossed by Santiago Carrillo, the General Secretary of the PCE, in his book
'Eurocommunism' and the State, published in April
1977, just before the Spanish parliamentary elections. In this work, Carrillo subjected Soviet
society to radical criticism, defining it as one of
"totalitarianism." According to him, the Soviet
system "has not been transformed; it has not been

116

made more democratic." A genuine workers' democracy "has not been realized anywhere, and least of all in the country which has been presented to us and still is being presented to us as the ideal model." Moreover, Carrillo argues, the Soviet regime has "retained many of its aspects of coercion in relations with the socialist states of the East, as was brought out with brutal clarity by the occupation of Czechoslovakia."[28]

Given Carrillo's explicit rejection of the validity of the Soviet model for any society, including that of the Soviet Union, Moscow's reaction was relatively slow in coming and surprisingly mild. This delay could probably be attributed to the indecision among the top party leadership on how most effectively to deal with Carrillo's challenge. One option would have been an instant and unconditional denouncement of Carrillo--a line that without doubt was advocated by the party ideologues. The other available option would have been simply to ignore the provocation. Either choice, however, would have constituted a significant gamble. Total silence on the part of Moscow might have been interpreted by both the Eurocommunist parties and by the Eastern European regimes as a sign of weakness, encouraging some and forcing others to adjust further their own position vis-à-vis the Soviet Union. On the other hand, any direct threat of excommunication would have carried with it another danger: if Carrillo did not recant, Moscow would have no choice but to carry its threat out in order not to lose face. In such a case, however, the French and Italian Communists would have been forced to stand behind the Spaniards, and the split between the Eurocommunist parties and Moscow would have been brought that much closer to becoming a reality. Furthermore, any immediate, though not necessarily unconditional attack on Carrillo would only have played into his hands, for it was he who had gambled that any confrontation with the Soviet leaders over his book would benefit his party at the elections.

Hence, instead of swiftly and officially denouncing the book, Moscow merely "reviewed" it in its weekly, New Times, on June 23, 1977--fully two months after it was published. The section dealing with how socialism should function in Western societies--the institutions of pluralistic democracy, the guarantee of basic civil rights, etc.--was totally passed over. Most of the review was devoted to what they described as Carrillo's attempt "to

117

discredit existing socialism...[and] the countries that have already created the new society, and primarily the Soviet Union."[29] However, even this, which can only be described as a defensive posture on the part of the Soviets, nevertheless seemed to frighten the Eastern European regimes a great deal. They feared that this war of words between Moscow and the PCE might result in other major Western European communist parties jumping to the defense of Carrillo. Such an eventuality could, in the end, lead to what all the Eastern European regimes feared the most: the creation of monocentric Eurocommunism.

It is significant that only the Czechoslovak press printed in full and discussed the New Times review the very same day it appeared in the Soviet Union. Initially, Bulgaria and East Germany merely printed a brief summary of the article without any comments of their own, waiting to fully publish the text of the Soviet attack for ten days. In Hungary, the New Times article was merely summarized in the regular press survey column on July 1, 1977. The Romanians did not so much as summarize the article at any time. Like the Yugoslav and the French and Italian Communist parties, they resolutely defended Carrillo's right to publish the book, even while stressing that they did not agree with its contents.[30] The only way that one can interpret Romania's reaction is to attribute its defense of Carrillo to the fear that otherwise the severity of the Soviet criticism of him might force not only the PCE, but also the PCI and the PCF into a rupture with the Soviet Union.

It is difficult to know with any certainty why the Soviets later toned down their criticism of Carrillo. Nothing is known about the top leadership debate on this issue, but judging from the way Moscow has handled the "Carrillo Affair," there must have been a significant degree of division within the Politburo. Whether because of this disunity or because of the silence among the Eastern European parties, or because of the negative reaction of the PCF and the PCI, [31] the Soviet press softened its accusations against Carrillo.[32]

Only after this partial retreat on the part of Moscow, did the Soviet bloc regimes (again with the exception of Romania which continued to support Carrillo, and of Czechoslovakia which sharply attacked Carrillo even before the Soviets did) begin to criticize Carrillo in their press.[33] However, in these articles, Carrillo was mainly accused of

118

"interfering in an inadmissible way into the internal affairs of the socialist countries," and for recommending to them his model of socialism. After this "episode," the Eastern European regimes muted their criticism. Again, an exception has been Czechoslovakia, where the attacks against Carrillo, the PCE, and against Eurocommunism in general, have continued unabated.[34]

Both the Eastern European reaction to the Soviet criticism of Carrillo, and the subsequent Soviet retreat, can be best explained in terms of their strong attempt to prevent the unification of the various "Eurocommunisms." The Bulgarian, the East German, and the Soviet leadership are reconciled to the existence of Eurocommunism as long as it does not harm the "prestige" of socialism in the Soviet Union and Eastern Europe. They all seem to assume that this eventuality will be minimized as long as Eurocommunism remains polycentric. Despite the cost of the ties which exist between its own dissidents and the Eurocommunist parties, even the Prague regime believes that it can coexist in the end with this form of Eurocommunism. Its continuous attacks on Eurocommunism, therefore, must not be seen as an attempt to "excommunicate" the Eurocommunist parties from the international communist movement, but merely as a ploy to discredit their "revisionist" ideology. Other Eastern European regimes hope to enlist Furocommunism in the defense of their autonomy vis-à-vis Moscow. However, for the reasons already dealt with, they all assume that they can do so only as long as Eurocommunism remains polycentric, that is, as long as it is neither ideologically nor strategically homogeneous. Specifically, these more independent Eastern European regimes seem to be aware that any anti-Moscow unity among the Eurocommunist parties would not only put an end to their own alignment with the Eurocommunists against the Soviet Union on certain issues, but could also undermine their domestic legitimacy.

Moscow is fully aware of the support that various Eurocommunist parties render to the Poles and the Hungarians, not to mention the Yugoslavs and the Romanians. However, it may well be deluding itself when it postulates that the negative effects of such support outweigh the negative consequences that would follow its rupture with Eurocommunism. A total break, though certainly costly, would deprive the more independent Eastern European regimes of allies and force them to realize that

119

their fate is firmly bound to that of the Soviet
Union. Without such a break, these regimes may
gradually and almost imperceptively (at first) de-
tach themselves from Moscow's control. Similarly,
the Soviet and Eastern European leaders underesti-
mate the threat of polycentric Eurocommunism for
the domestic stability of their regimes. There is
a significant amount of available evidence which
suggests that even the most conservative Eastern
European regimes have been toning down their repressive policies in order not to further stimulate
criticism on the part of the Eurocommunist press.
These changes have been extremely gradual and nearly imperceptible. However, instead of placating
the opposition forces, they have only tended to increase their activities further.

Despite what is commonly believed in the West,
the reactions of all the Eastern European regimes
to these heightened dissident activities have re-
sulted, to a large extent, in a further softening
of their domestic policies. In both Poland and
Hungary, the success of the tenuous relationship
with Eurocommunism is further complicated by the
fact that the top leaders make use of it not only
in dealing with Moscow but also in isolating some
of their own more conservative colleagues. Thus,
in these countries, besides encouraging political
dissidence in the society as a whole, Eurocommunism
adds to the intra-elite frictions as well. The
same may soon become true in other Eastern European
countries.[35]

In sum, Eurocommunism has the capacity to "in-
fect" the whole network of internal and bloc relations. How precisely this "infection" will, in the
end, affect the internal situation within each
country and bloc unity as a whole, is impossible to
predict at this point. However, the fact remains
that as long as Eurocommunism remains polycentric,
its impact on Eastern Europe can only be debilitat-
ing, that is, it will gradually but inevitably undermine the established forms of both internal and
bloc political control. A reversal in the course of
this "disease" could only come about through drastic
means. Assuming the permanence of the Eurocommunist
phenomenon, the only way its infection of the Eastern European countries could be dealt with effectively is through its isolation: by their clear
break with Eurocommunism. However, given its present usefulness for many of these regimes, it is unlikely that they themselves would initiate this
rupture. In the end, the insidious disease of

polycentric Eurocommunism must first be detected by Moscow before Eastern Europe can be "successfully" treated for it.

FOOTNOTES

1. The Leftist parties received 49.25% of the vote as opposed to 50.75% for the parties associated with the Center-right government coalition.
2. Pravda, Moscow, March 24, 1978, p. 5.
3. Za rubezhom, no. 10, 1978, pp. 7-8.
4. Kevin Devlin, "Spanish Communist Party to Break with Leninism," RFE, RAD Background, November 28, 1977.
5. Quoted in Henry Tanner, "Italian Reds Hold Parley and Insist on a Cabinet Role," New York Times, January 27, 1978.
6. For a more detailed analysis of the PCF's "transformation," see for example, Neil Nugent and David Lowe, "The French Communist Party: The Road to Democratic Government?" The Political Quarterly, 48(3), July-September 1977, pp. 270-87.
7. Le Monde, September 23, 1977.
8. Ibid., September 24, 1977.
9. Victor Zorza, "Europe's Communists: A Hex from the Kremlin?" Washington Post, September 21, 1977.
10. For a description of the PCF's Eurocommunist position as "Gaullocommunism" see Ronald Tiersky, "French Communism, Eurocommunism and Soviet Power," in Rudolf L. Tökés, ed., Eurocommunism and Détente (New York: New York University Press, 1978).
11. This does not mean that the Soviet leaders have accepted the "term" Eurocommunism.
12. See for example, Kevin Devlin, "The Challenge of Eurocommunism," Problems of Communism, 25(1), January-February 1977, pp. 1-20.
13. See for example the interview with V. Afanasyev on the Spanish Communist Party Congress in Rudé Právo, Praha, April 26, 1978.
14. Furthermore, any ideological war with "Eurocommunism" as a whole, would in all likelihood lead to ideological confrontation with "Afrocommunism" and "Asiocommunism."
15. I am referring here to the Soviet attack on Santiago Carrillo's book 'Eurocommunism' and the State, in New Times, June 23, 1977. For the Italian, French, and Belgian defense of the General Secretary of the Spanish Communist party, see

l'Unità, l'Humanité, and Le Drapeau Rouge of June
24, 1977.

16. For a somewhat more detailed analysis of
the differences in attitudes of Eastern European
regimes towards Eurocommunism and the social and
political forces responsible for them, see, for
example, my "Eastern Europe, Eurocommunism and the
Problems of Détente" in Morton A. Kaplan, ed., The
Many Faces of Communism (New York: The Free Press,
1978).

17. Since the fall of 1976, the Czechoslovak
leadership has been challenged by the signatories
of Charter 77 whose demand for "civil rights" reflects ideological kinship with the Eurocommunist
parties. Subsequent harrassment, arrests, and
trials of some of the civil rights campaigners by
the Czechoslovak authorities have been instantly
denounced in the Eurocommunist press. As an example
of the recent PCF criticism of political repression
in Czechoslovakia, see Marchais' reply to a letter
sent to him by Aleš Lederer, son of the imprisoned
Czechoslovak journalist Jiří Lederer in l'Humanité,
December 19, 1977.

18. Todor Zhivkov, "A Year of Peace, a Year of
Struggle," Problems of Peace and Socialism, December 1976.

19. L'Unità, February 10, 1978.

20. See for example, Kevin Devlin, "The Challenge of Eurocommunism," Problems of Communism,
25(1), January-February 1977, pp. 1-20.

21. Le Monde, February 6, 1976.

22. Moderate Eurocommunist ideology can also
be useful to both Janos Kádár and Edward Gierek,
the Hungarian and Polish party leaders, in dealing
with their more conservative colleagues.

23. Janos Kádár, "On Several Hungarian Experiences in the Building of Socialism," Problems of
Peace and Socialism (the Hungarian language edition), January 1977.

24. Tribuna Lundu, August 3, 1977.

25. In 1977 alone, three top party meetings
took place between the Poles and the Italians. On
March 23, the Secretary of the PUWP, Rysard Frelek,
talked with the PCI Secretariat member Gian Carlo
Pajeta in Rome. On November 17, Sergio Segre
visited Warsaw. Finally, during his visit to the
Italian government from November 28-30, Edward
Gierek, the Polish party chief, had a meeting with
Enrico Berlinguer. There were two top party meetings between the Hungarians and the Italians in
1977, one during Kádár's visit to Rome in July and

the other during Berlinguer's visit to Budapest in October.

26. For the criticism in the Eurocommunist press of the repressive aspects of the Polish regime, see e.g., l'Unità, May 21 and 26, 1977; Rinascita, May 27, 1977.

27. Janos Kádár, op.cit. Indications are that there has been some opposition to this tolerant view of Eurocommunism on the part of some top party members. In the September 1976 issue of the Problems of Peace and Socialism, Dezso Nemes, a member of the Politburo of the Hungarian party, attacked the position of the Eurocommunist parties by claiming that any socialist regime must "perform the historic function of the dictatorship of the proletariat."

28. Santiago Carrillo, 'Eurocommunism' and the State (London: Lawrence and Wishart, 1977), pp. 156-59.

29. "Contrary to the Interests of Peace and Socialism in Europe: Concerning the Book of 'Eurocommunism' and the State by Santiago Carrillo," New Times (English language edition), June 23, 1977. It seems to me that Moscow makes distinction between "autonomous analysis" and hostile criticism.

30. Scinteia, July 5, 1977; see also the Washington Post, July 8, 1977, interview with Nicolae Ceausescu, the Romanian leader. In this interview, Ceausescu reiterated the Romanian position on Moscow's attack on Carrillo, stating that "the criticism made by the Soviet review was unjust and [did] not conform to the type of relations that should exist between communist parties."

31. Moscow retracted its hard-line position against Carrillo on July 8, 1978--one week after top party talks took place between the PCSU and the PCI. The Italians reportedly told the Soviet leaders that they have the right to criticize Carrillo's book, but that their condemnation of him as "an enemy of socialism" was "not acceptable." l'Unità, July 5, 1977.

32. "Putting the Record Straight," New Times (English language edition), July 8, 1977. Subsequent Soviet behavior is even stranger. In October 1977, Victor Afanasyev, a member of the Soviet party's Central Committee and editor of the party newspaper Pravda, invited Carrillo to speak in Moscow at ceremonies marking the sixtieth anniversary of the October Revolution. Afanasyev told Carrillo that Brezhnev wanted to reduce tension between the two parties and to open discussions on theoretical

differences raised in his book 'Eurocommunism' and the State. (See Miguel Acoca, "Spanish, Soviet Communists Seen Reaching a Truce," Washington Post, October 24, 1977, p. 33.) However, once in Moscow, the Soviet authorities refused to let Carrillo deliver even a fairly moderate speech. On the other hand, Enrico Berlinguer was not only allowed to deliver his speech (one very similar to Carrillo's), but was even received later by Brezhnev. This suggests that even though Brezhnev may personally prefer a softer line vis-à-vis the Eurocommunist parties, he is, on occasion, outvoted by his more ideological colleagues.

33. See for example Nepszabadsag, July 27, 1977 and Tribuna Ludu, August 7, 1977.

34. The latest Czechoslovak strong attack on Eurocommunism appeared in Rude´ Právo on December 15, 1978.

35. See my "Eastern Europe, Eurocommunism and the Problems of Detente," op.cit., especially pp. 237-53.